PIANO • VOCAL • GUITAR

KENNY G GREATEST HITS

CONTENTS

2	songbird
5	silhouette
10	forever in love
14	everytime i close my eyes (with Babyface)
18	sentimental
23	the moment
27	how could an angel break my heart (with Toni Braxton)
32	loving you
37	you send me (with Michael Bolton)
42	going home
45	havana
51	by the time this night is over (with Peabo Bryson)
57	baby g
61	don't make me wait for love
66	theme from <u>dying young</u>
70	all the way / one for my baby (and one more for the road) (with Frank Sinatra)
78	innocence

Photography by Matthew Rolston

ISBN 0-7935-9333-6

7777 W. BLUEMOUND RD. P.O. BOX 13819 MILWAUKEE, WI 53213

For all works contained herein:
Unauthorized copying, arranging, adapting, recording or public performance is an infringement of copyright.
Infringers are liable under the law.

Visit Hal Leonard Online at
www.halleonard.com

SONGBIRD

By KENNY G

Slowly, lyrically

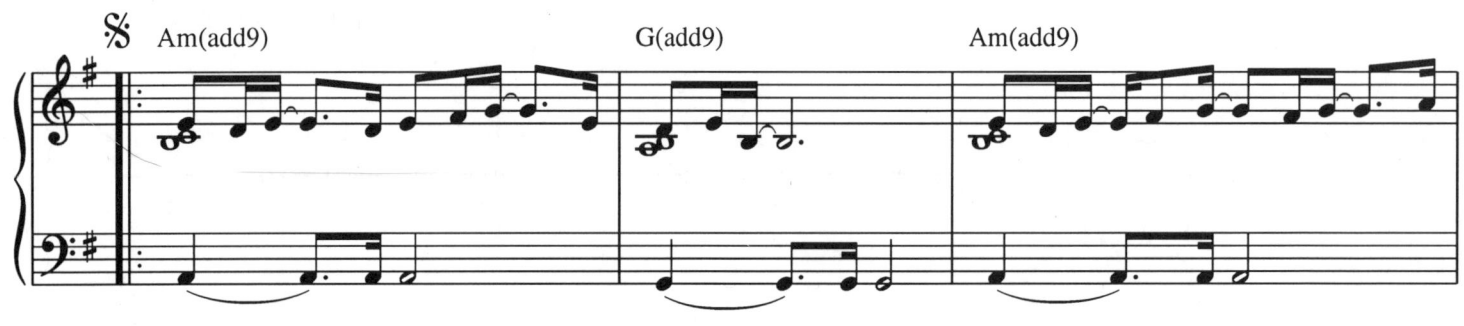

© 1986 EMI BLACKWOOD MUSIC INC., KUZU MUSIC, KENNY G MUSIC and HIGH TECH MUSIC
All Rights for KUZU MUSIC Controlled and Administered by EMI BLACKWOOD MUSIC INC.
All Rights Reserved   International Copyright Secured   Used by Permission

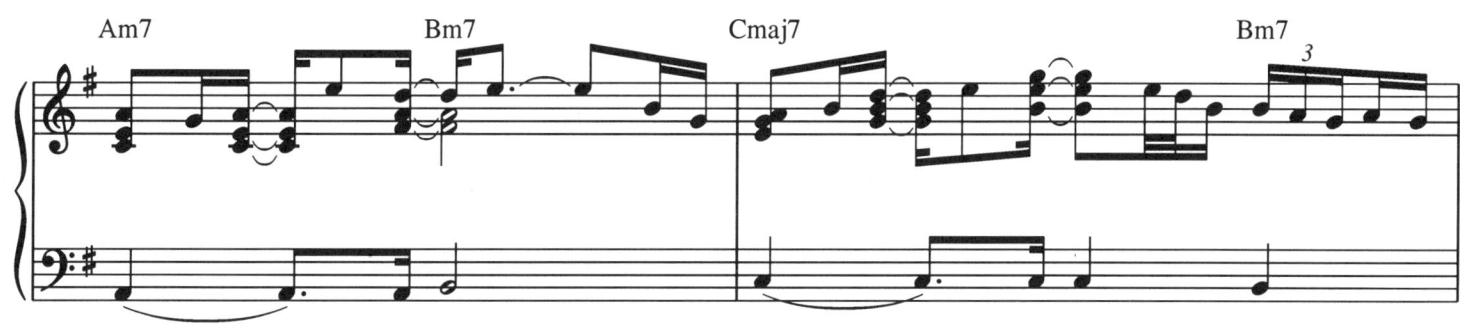

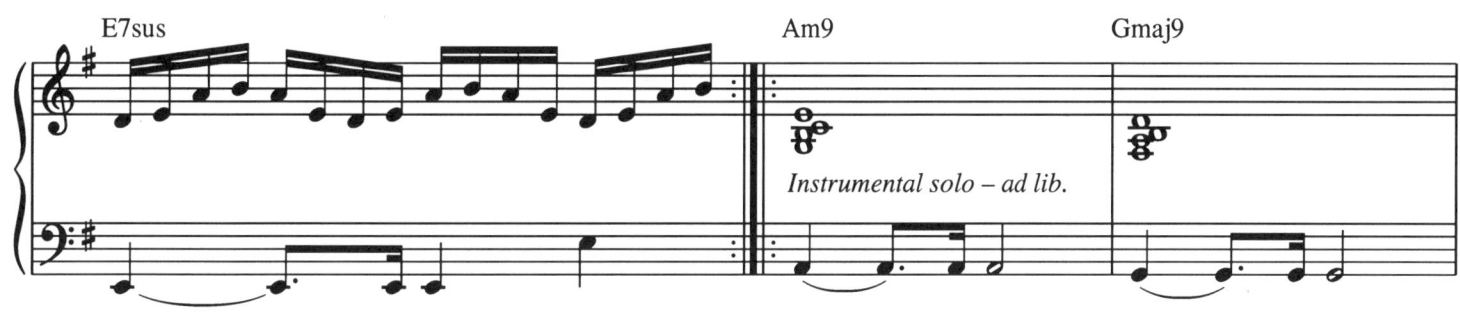
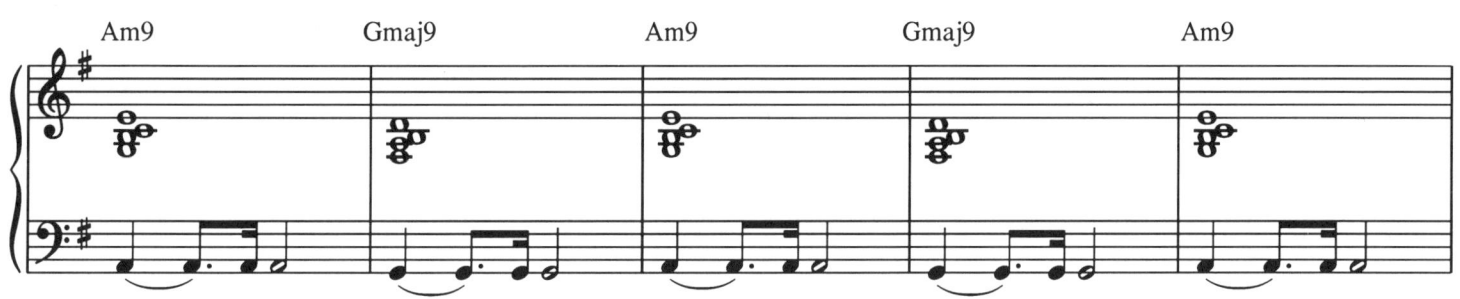

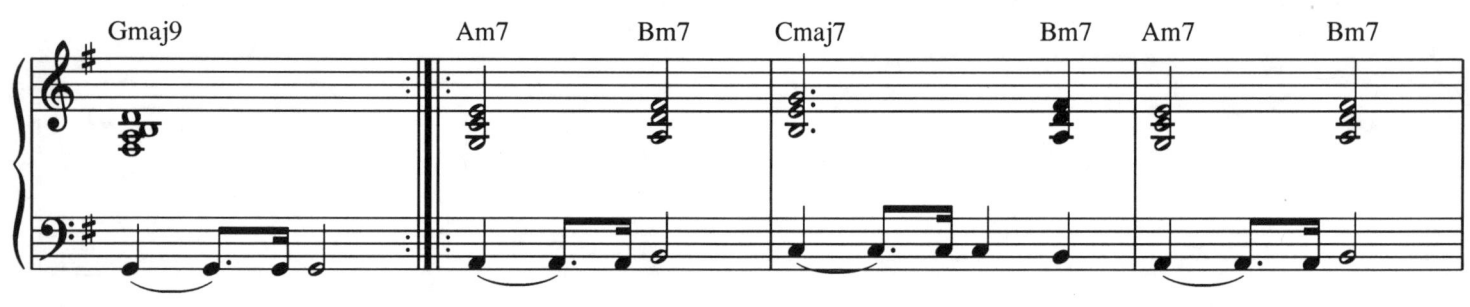
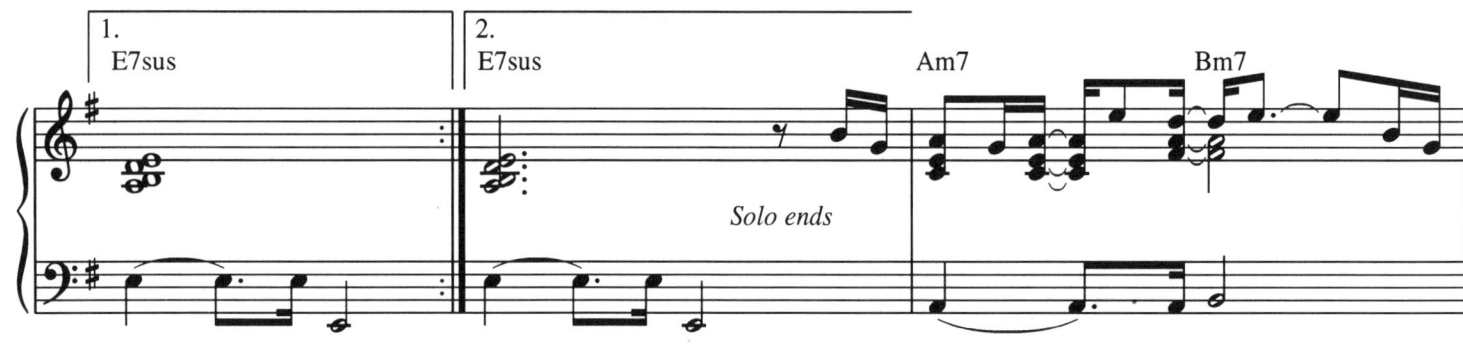
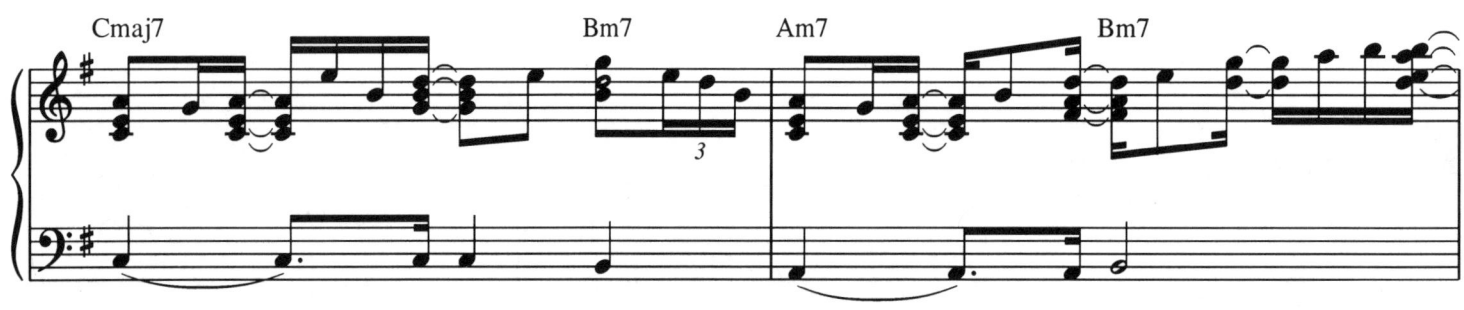

SILHOUETTE

By KENNY G

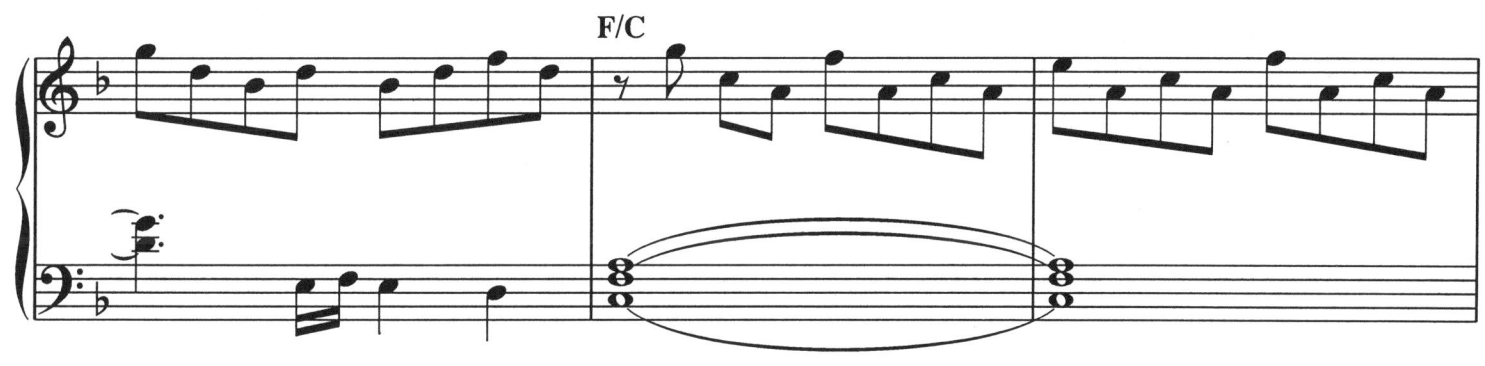

© 1988 EMI Blackwood Music Inc., KUZU Music, KENNY G MUSIC and HIGH TECH MUSIC
All Rights for KUZU MUSIC Controlled and Administered by EMI BLACKWOOD MUSIC INC.
All Rights Reserved   International Copyright Secured   Used by Permission

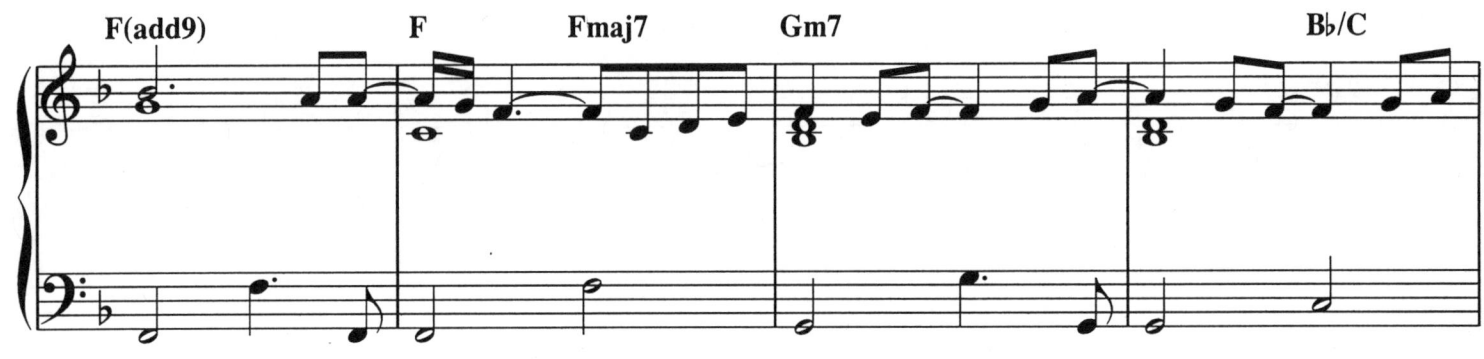

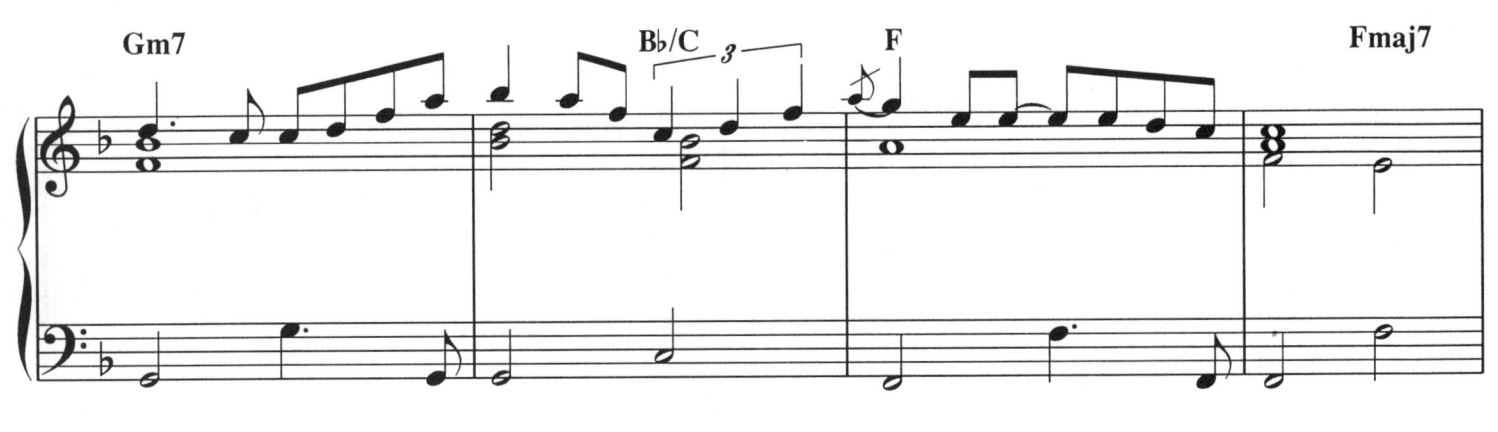

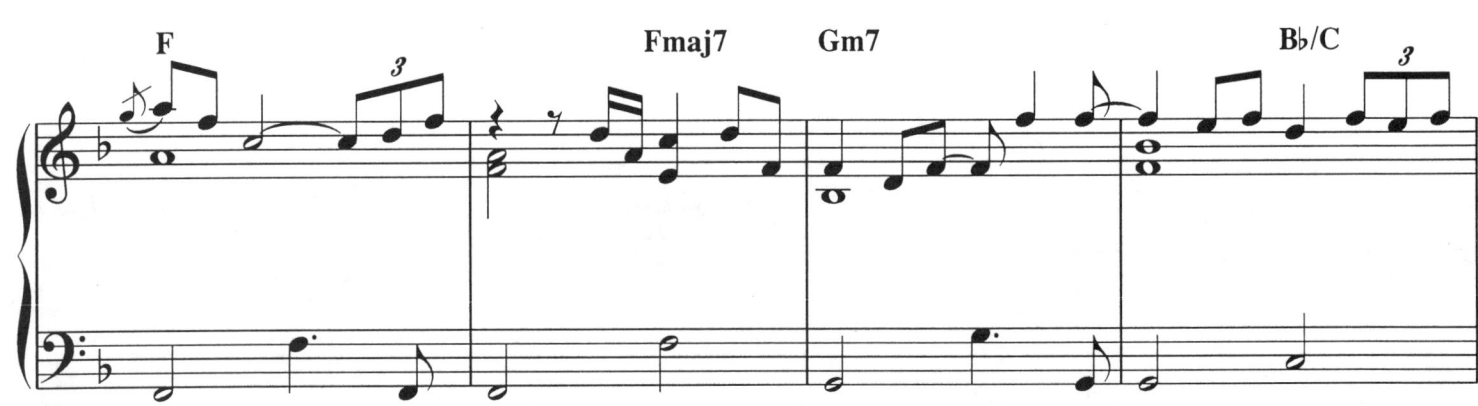

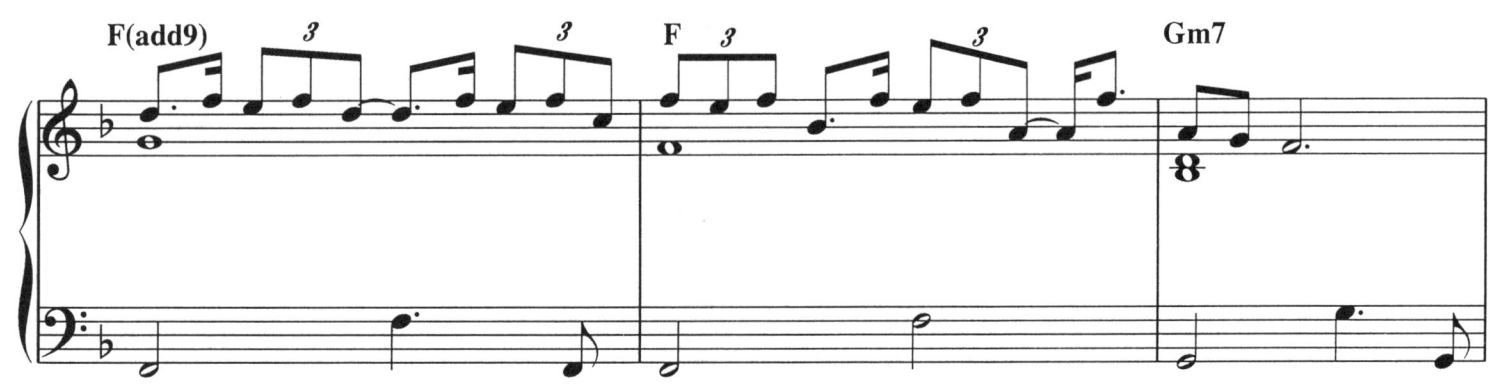
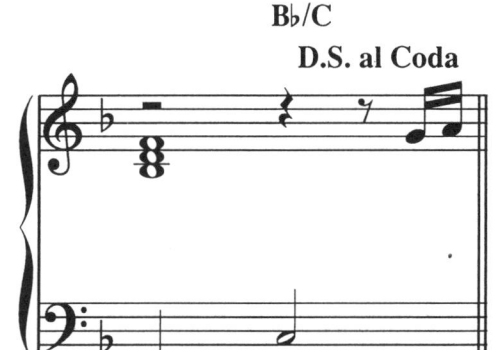

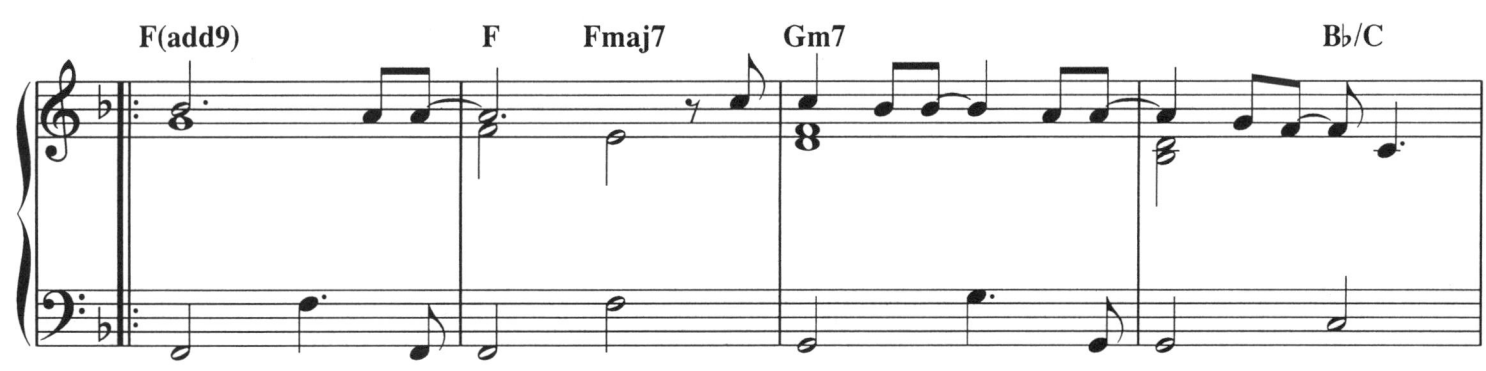

FOREVER IN LOVE

By KENNY G

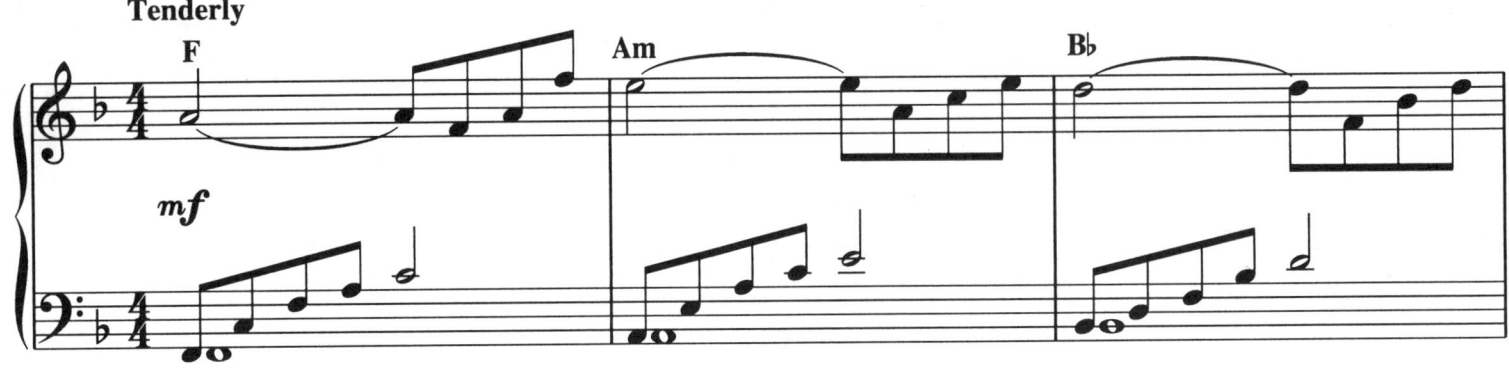
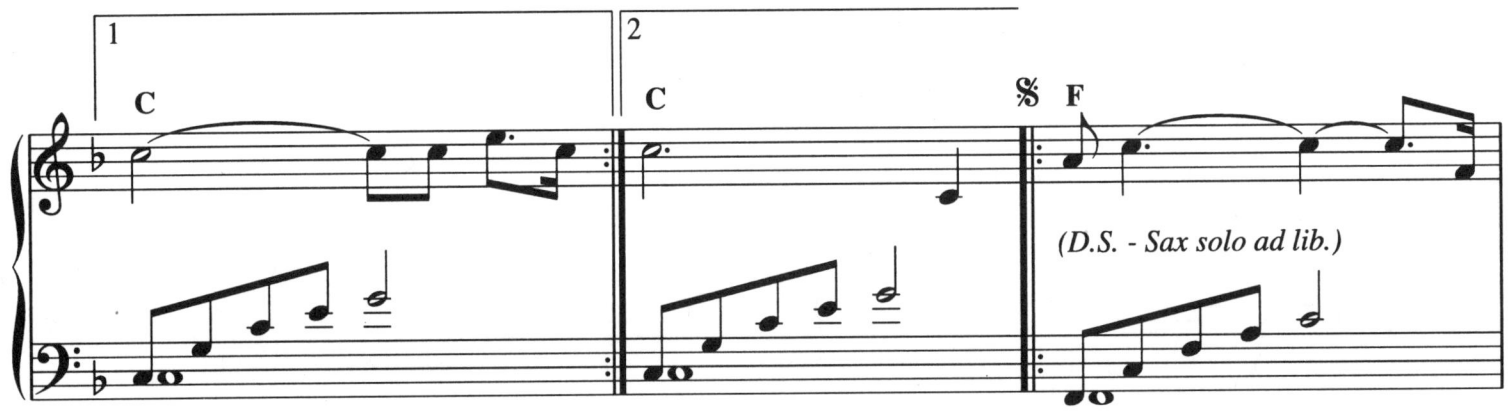

© 1992 EMI BLACKWOOD MUSIC INC., KUZU MUSIC, KENNY G MUSIC and HIGH TECH MUSIC
All Rights for KUZU MUSIC Controlled and Administered by EMI BLACKWOOD MUSIC INC.
All Rights Reserved   International Copyright Secured   Used by Permission

SENTIMENTAL

By KENNY G
and WALTER AFANASIEFF

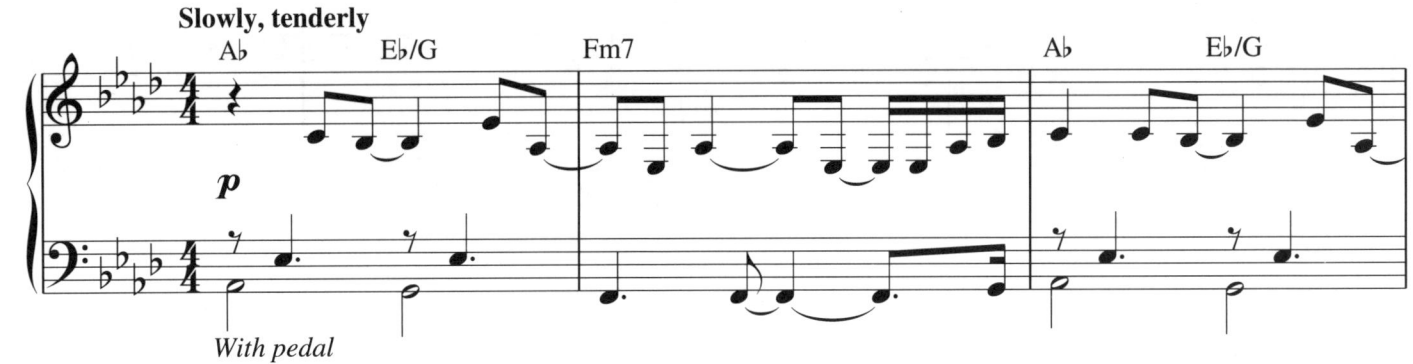
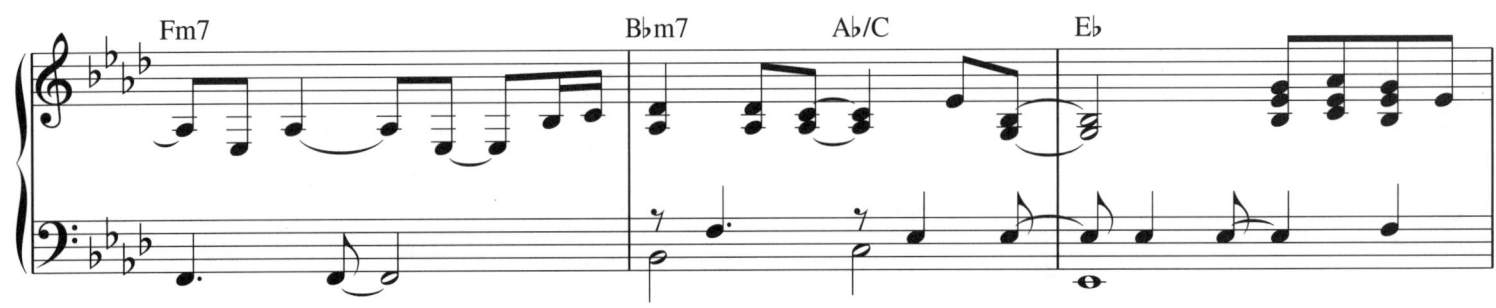
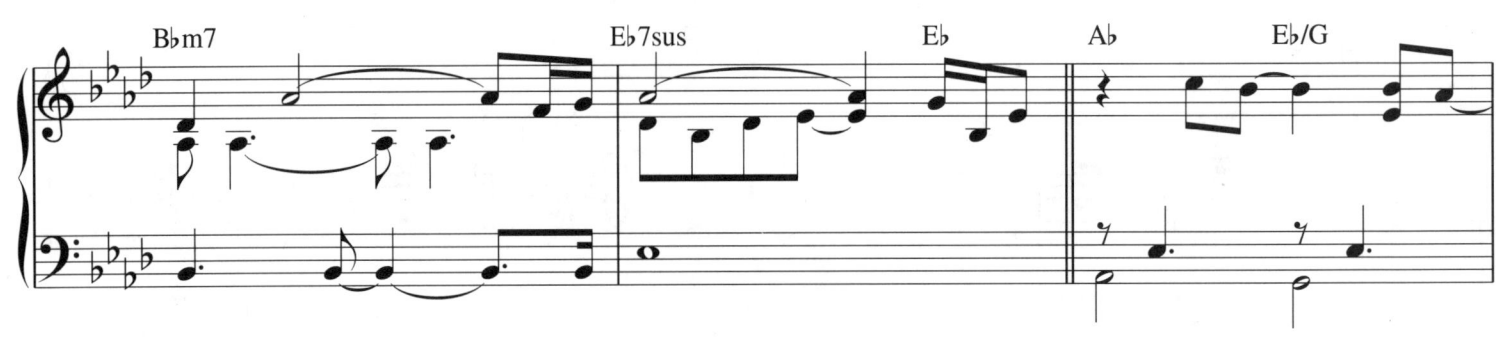
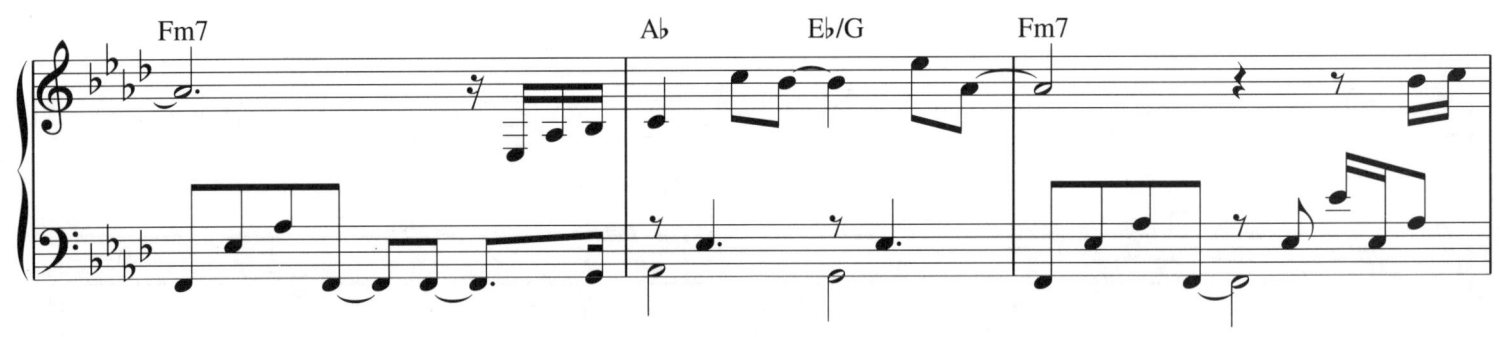

© 1992 EMI BLACKWOOD MUSIC INC., KUZU MUSIC, KENNY G MUSIC, HIGH TECH MUSIC, WB MUSIC CORP. and WALLYWORLD MUSIC
All Rights for KUZU MUSIC Controlled and Administered by EMI BLACKWOOD MUSIC INC.
All Rights for WALLYWORLD MUSIC Administered by WB MUSIC CORP.
All Rights Reserved   International Copyright Secured   Used by Permission

THE MOMENT

By KENNY G

HOW COULD AN ANGEL BREAK MY HEART

Words and Music by BABYFACE
and TONI BRAXTON

LOVING YOU

By KENNY G,
WALTER AFANASIEFF and DAN SHEA

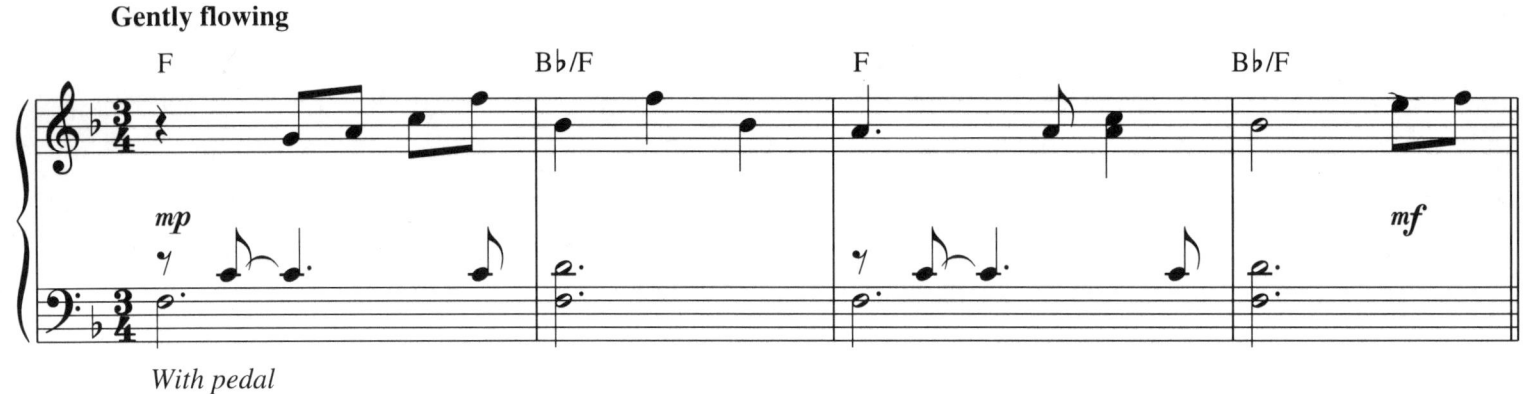
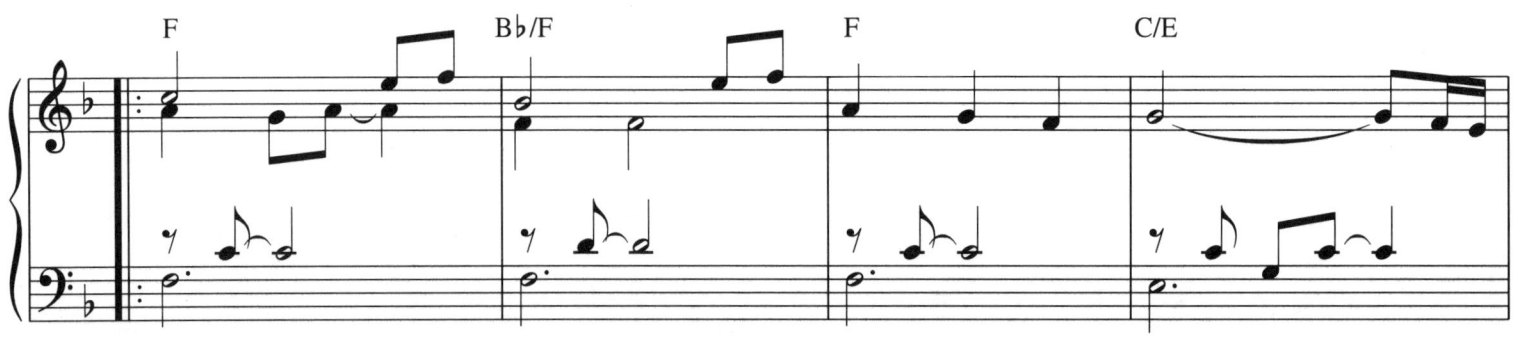
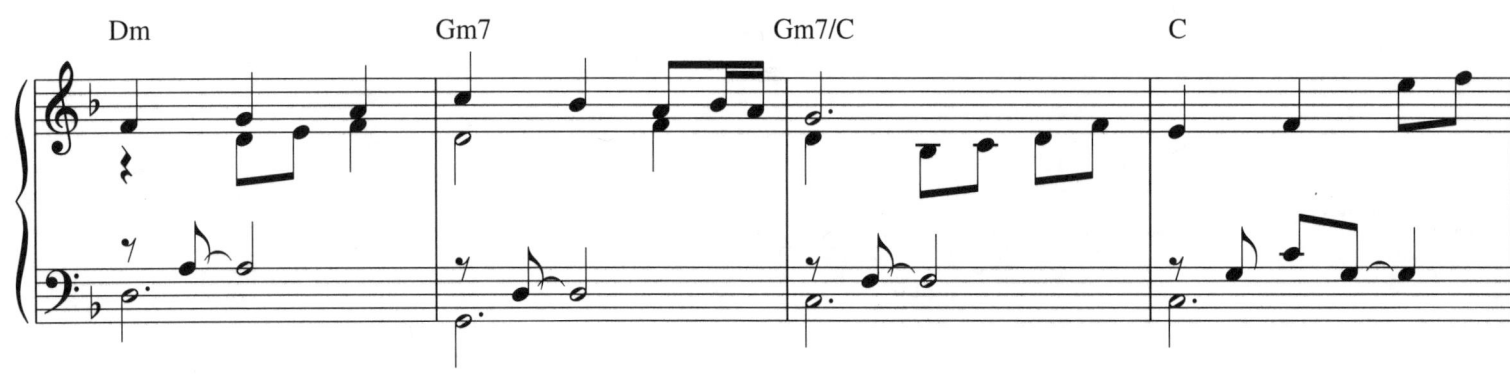
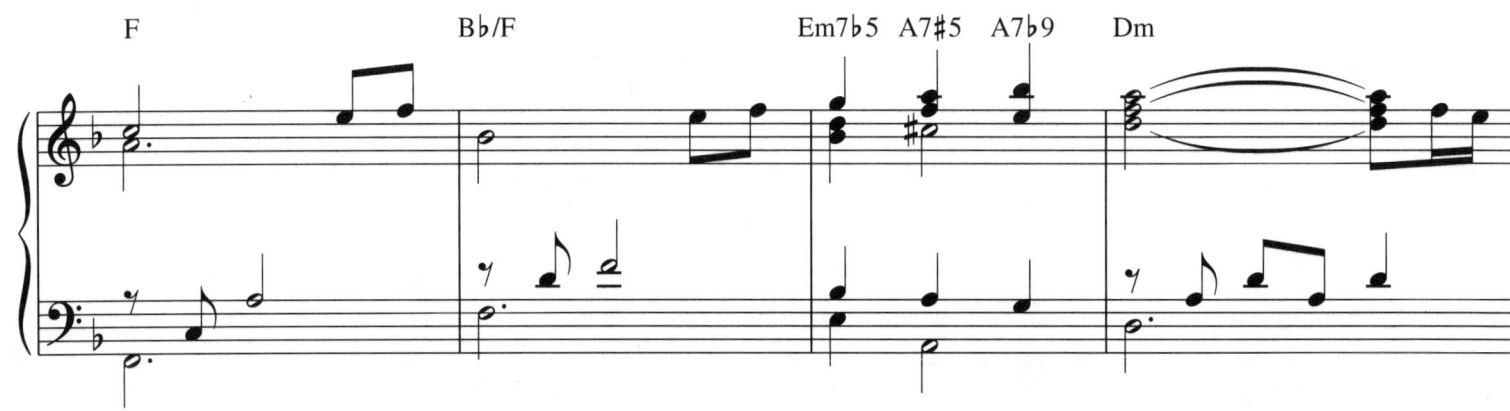

© 1997 KENNY G MUSIC, SONY/ATV TUNES LLC, WALLYWORLD MUSIC and PICNIC HILL MUSIC
All Rights on behalf of SONY/ATV TUNES LLC and WALLYWORLD MUSIC Administered by SONY/ATV MUSIC PUBLISHING, 8 Music Square West, Nashville, TN 37203
International Copyright Secured   All Rights Reserved

YOU SEND ME

Words and Music by
SAM COOKE

GOING HOME

By KENNY G
and WALTER AFANASIEFF

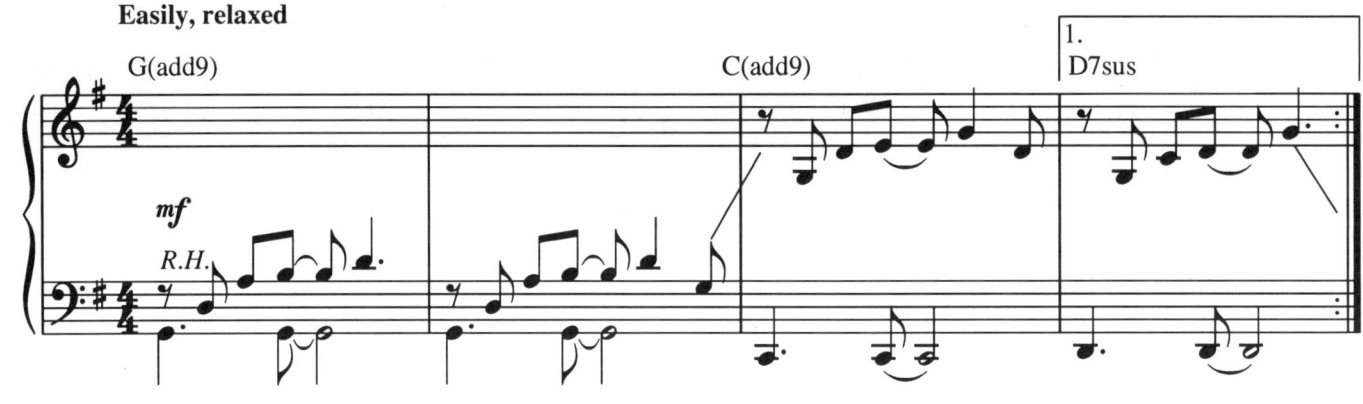

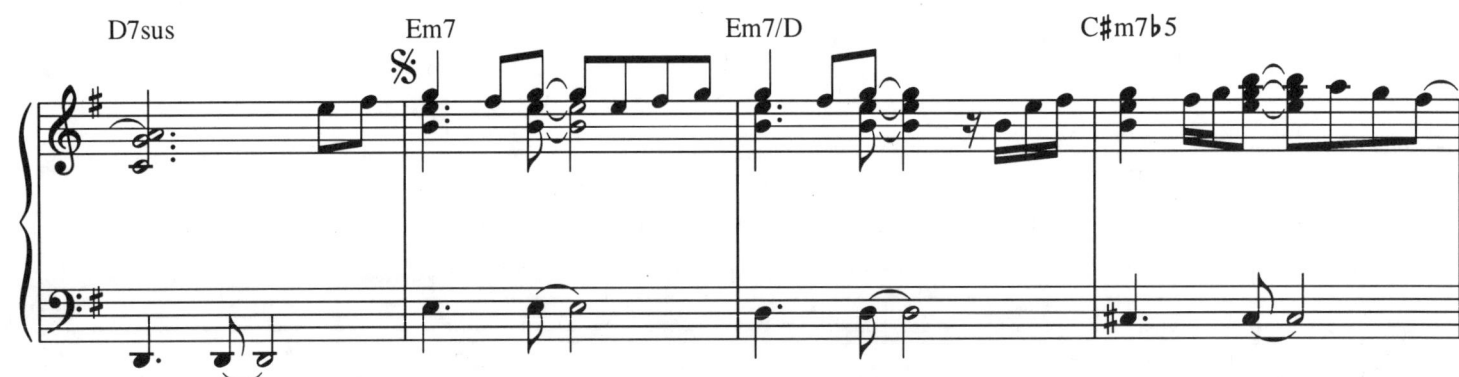

© 1989 EMI BLACKWOOD MUSIC INC., KUZU MUSIC, KENNY G MUSIC, HIGH TECH MUSIC and WALLYWORLD MUSIC
All Rights for KUZU MUSIC Controlled and Administered by EMI BLACKWOOD MUSIC INC.
All Rights for WALLYWORLD MUSIC Administered by WB MUSIC CORP.
All Rights Reserved   International Copyright Secured   Used by Permission

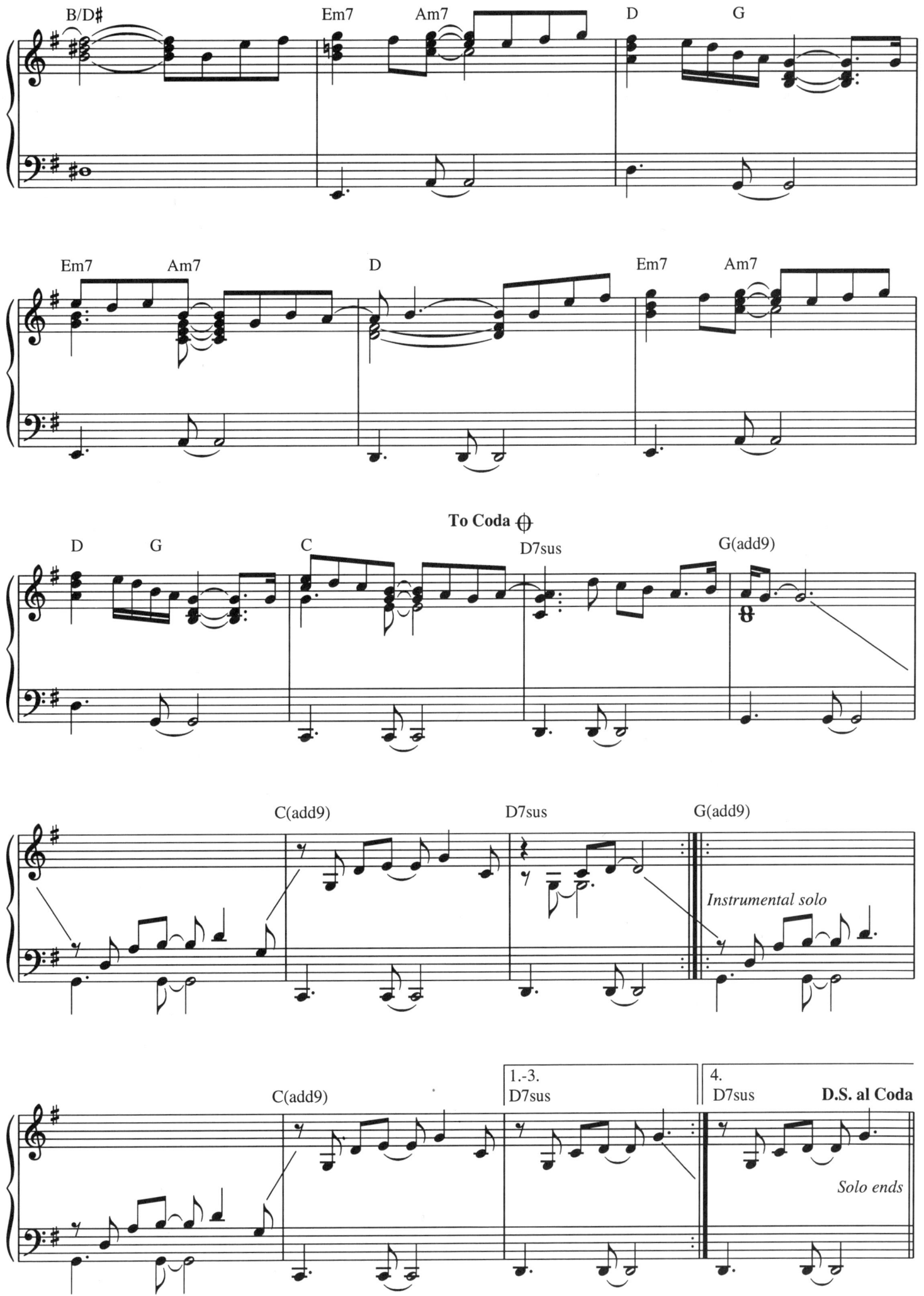

HAVANA

By KENNY G
and WALTER AFANASIEFF

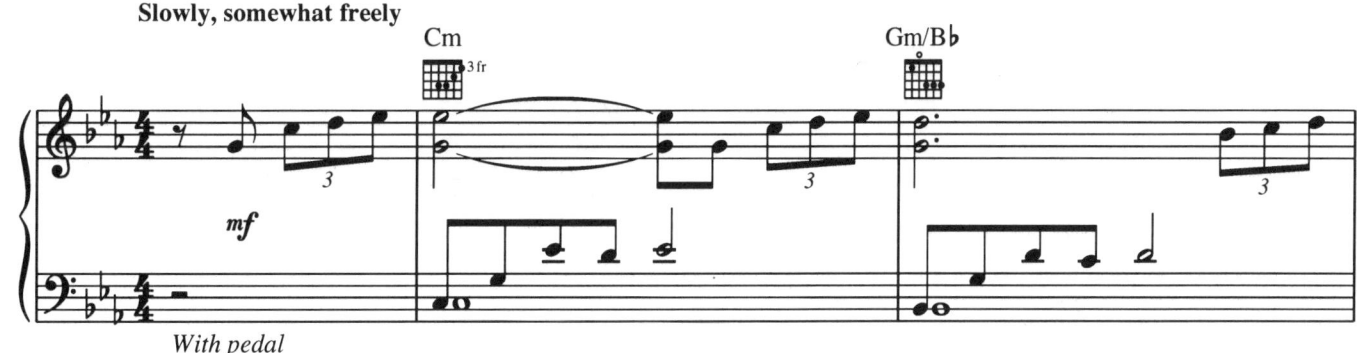
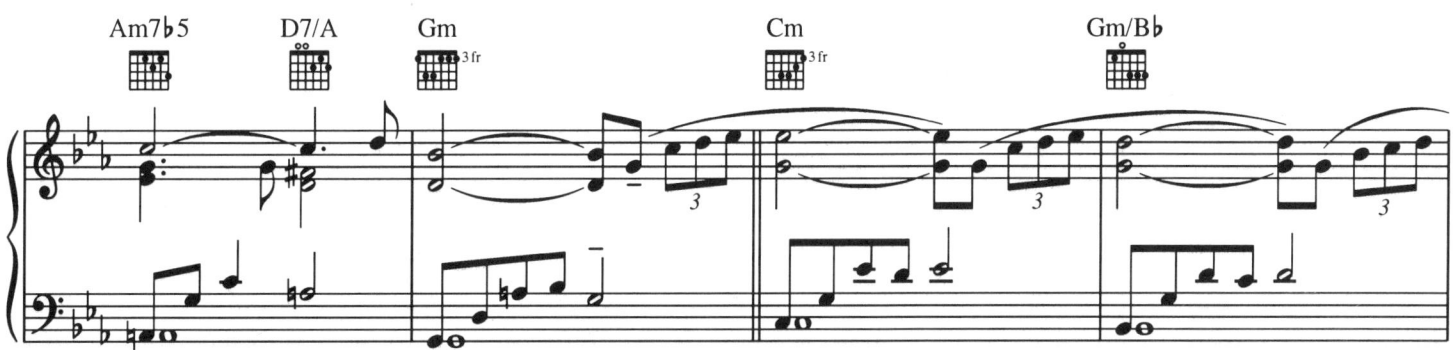
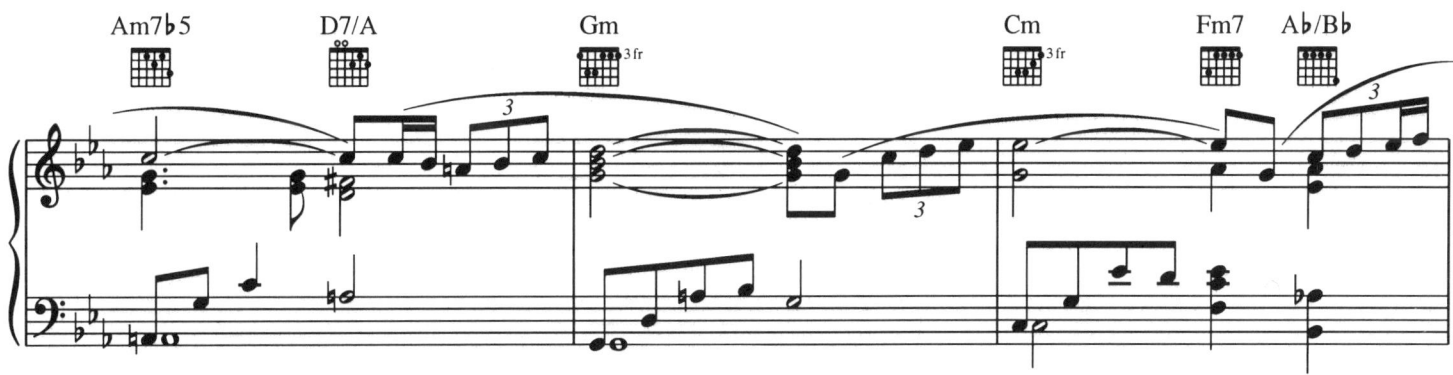
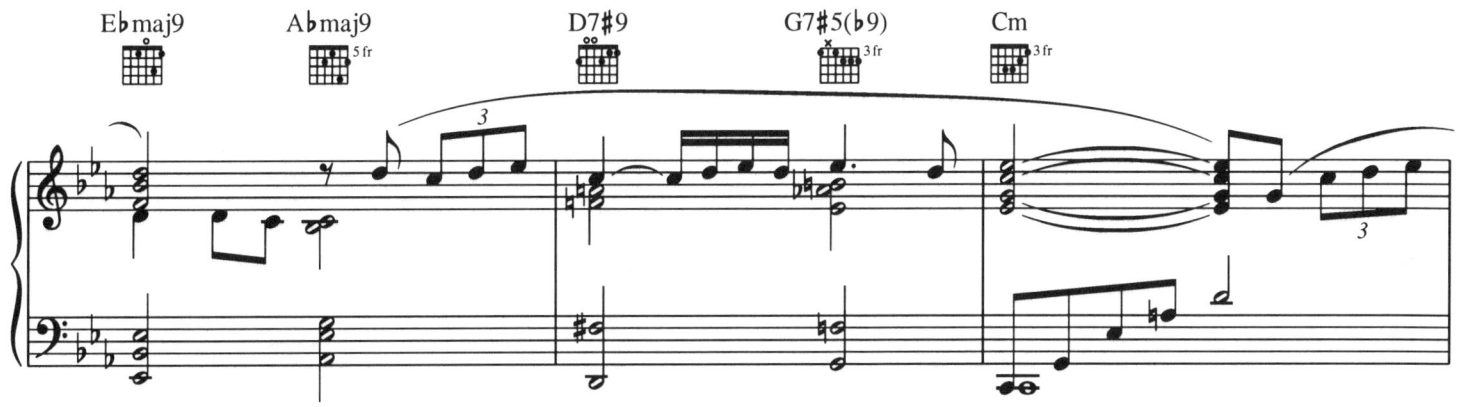

© 1996 KENNY G MUSIC, SONY/ATV TUNES LLC and WALLYWORLD MUSIC
All Rights on behalf of SONY/ATV TUNES LLC and WALLYWORLD MUSIC Administered by SONY/ATV MUSIC PUBLISHING, 8 Music Square West, Nashville, TN 37203
International Copyright Secured   All Rights Reserved

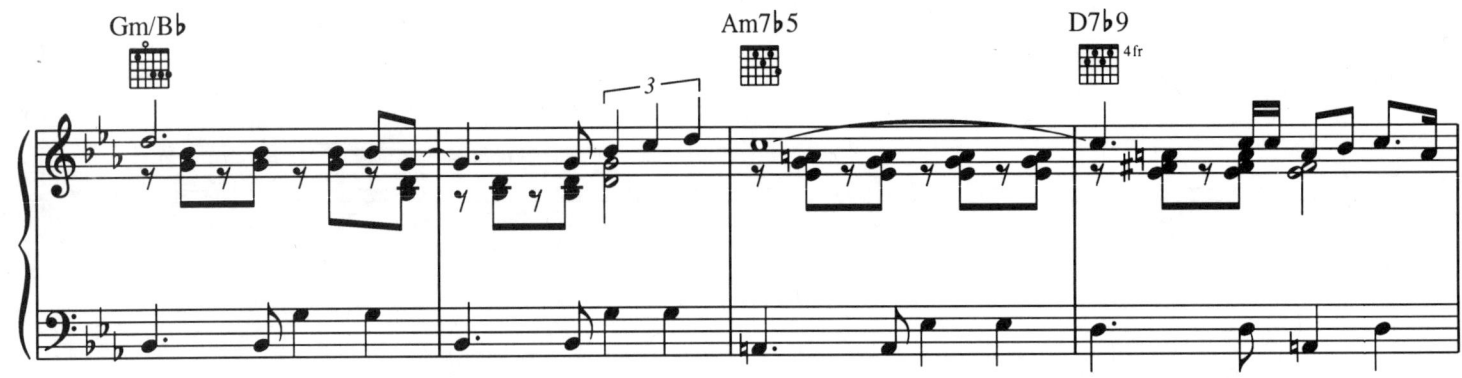

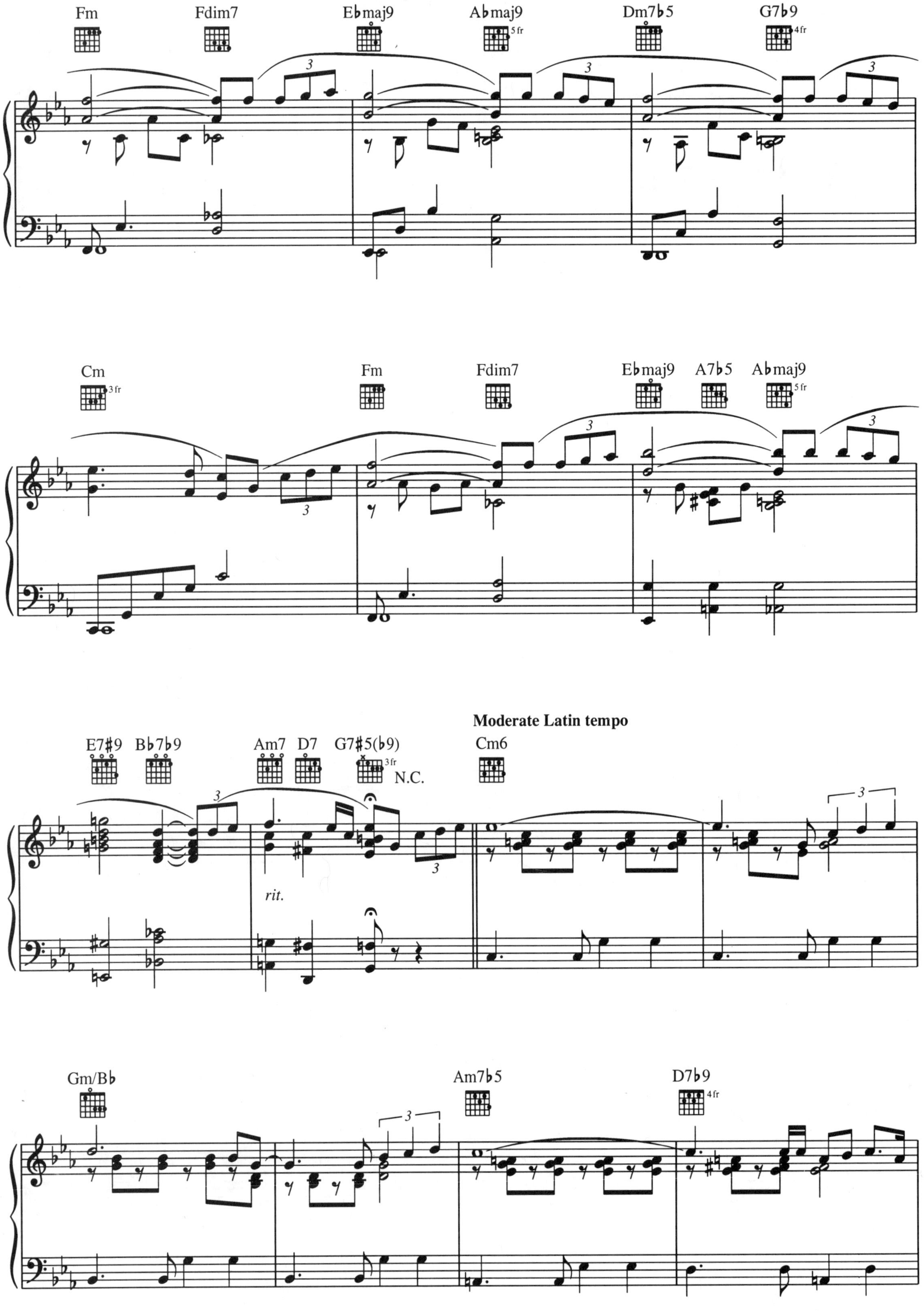
Fm
Fdim7
E♭maj9
A♭maj9
Dm7♭5
G7♭9
Cm
Fm
Fdim7
E♭maj9
A7♭5
A♭maj9
E7♯9
B♭7♭9
Am7
D7
G7♯5(♭9)
N.C.
rit.
Moderate Latin tempo
Cm6
Gm/B♭
Am7♭5
D7♭9

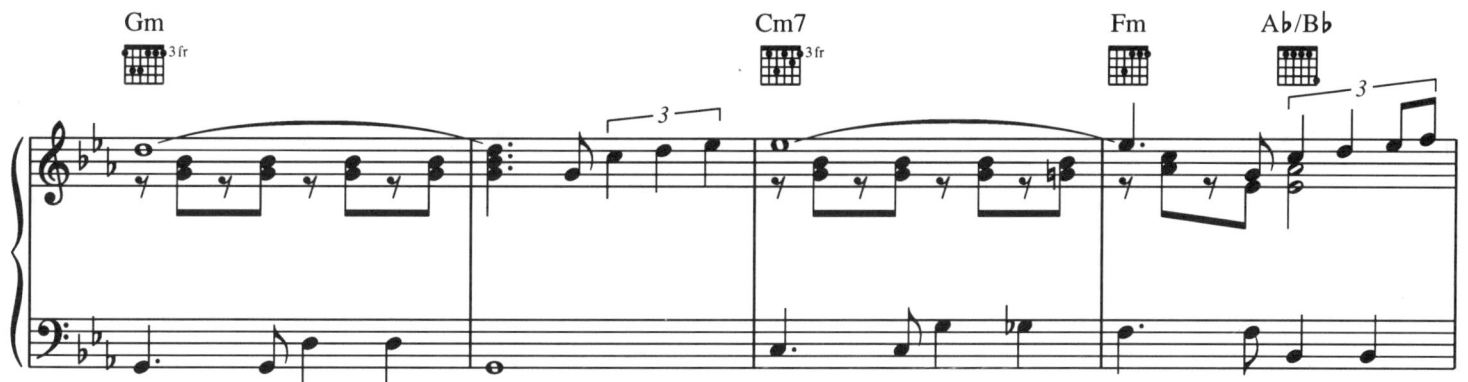
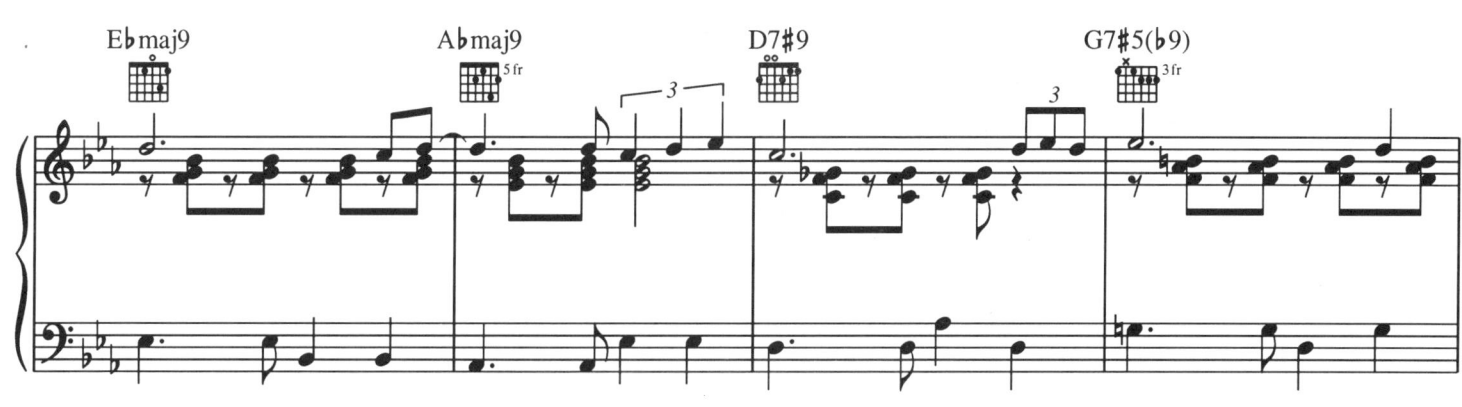
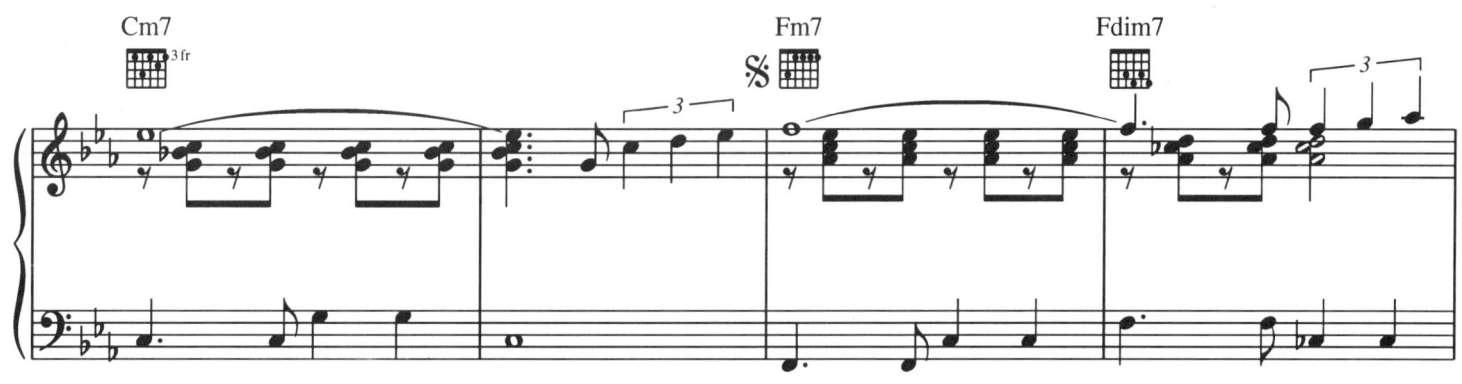
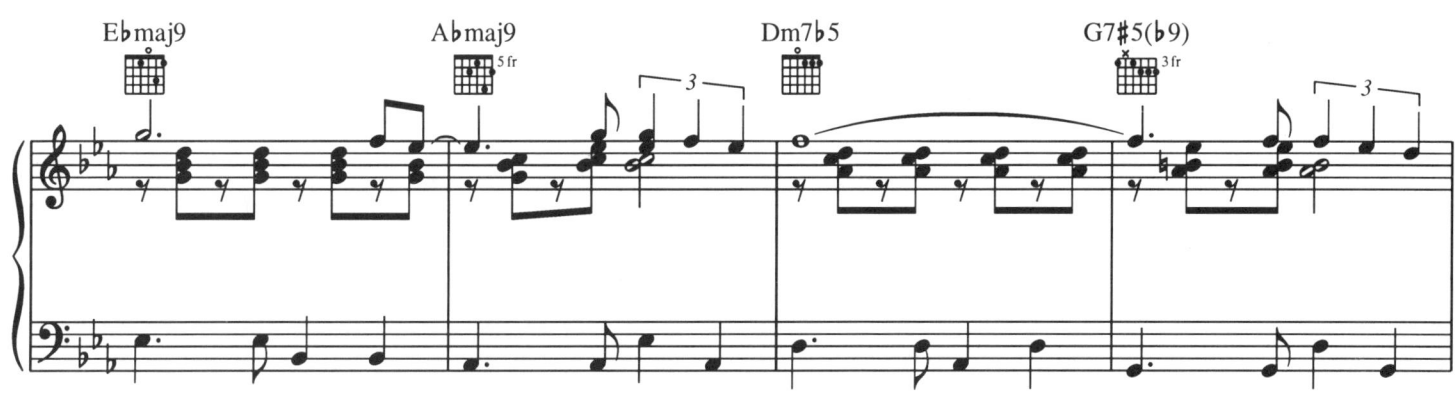

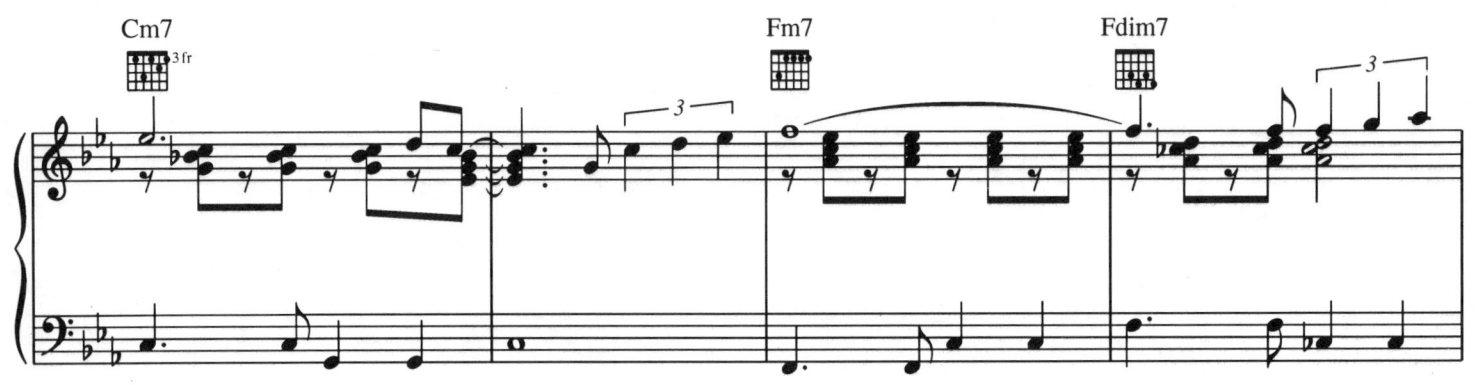
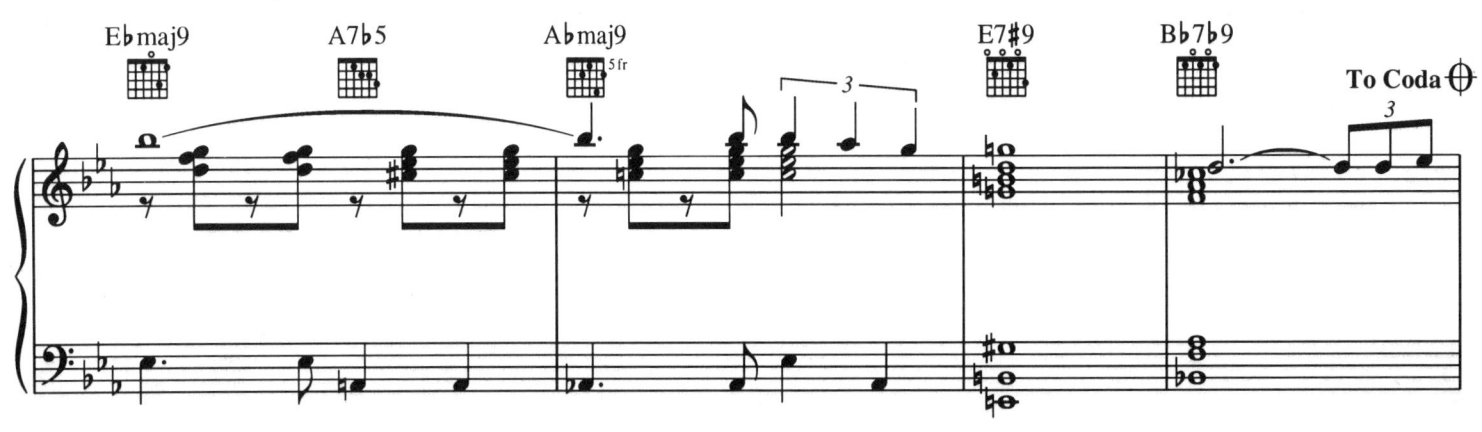
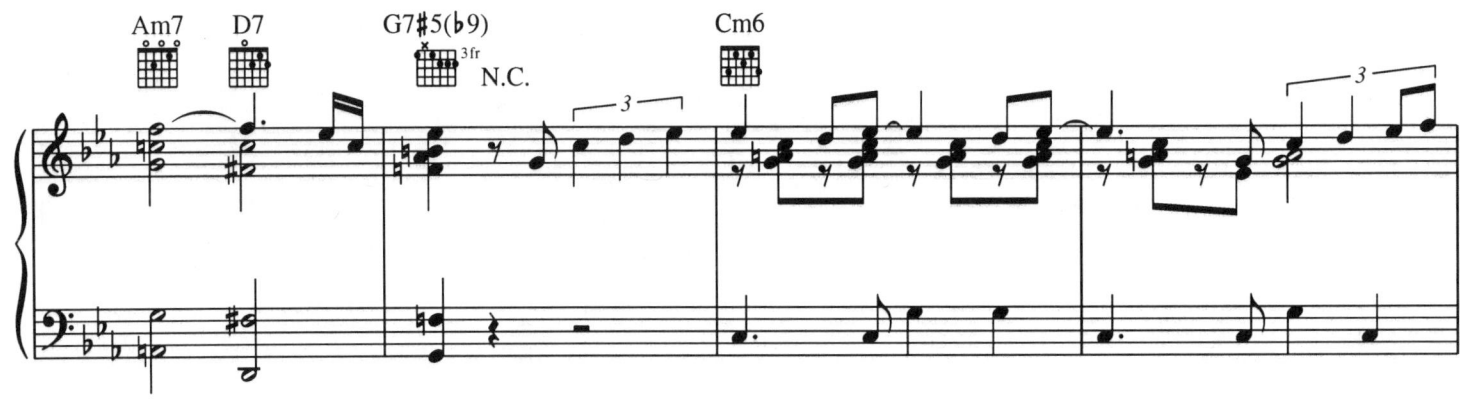
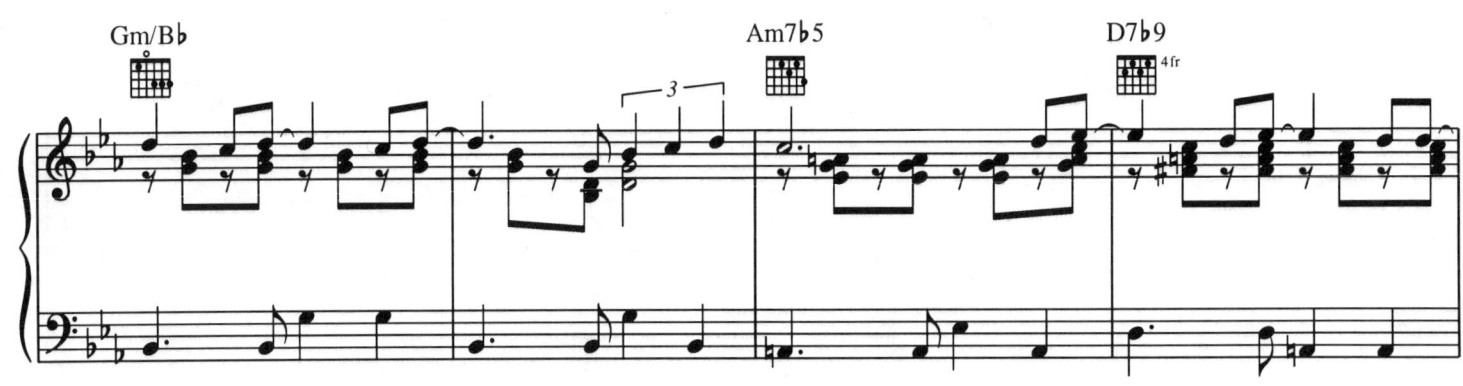

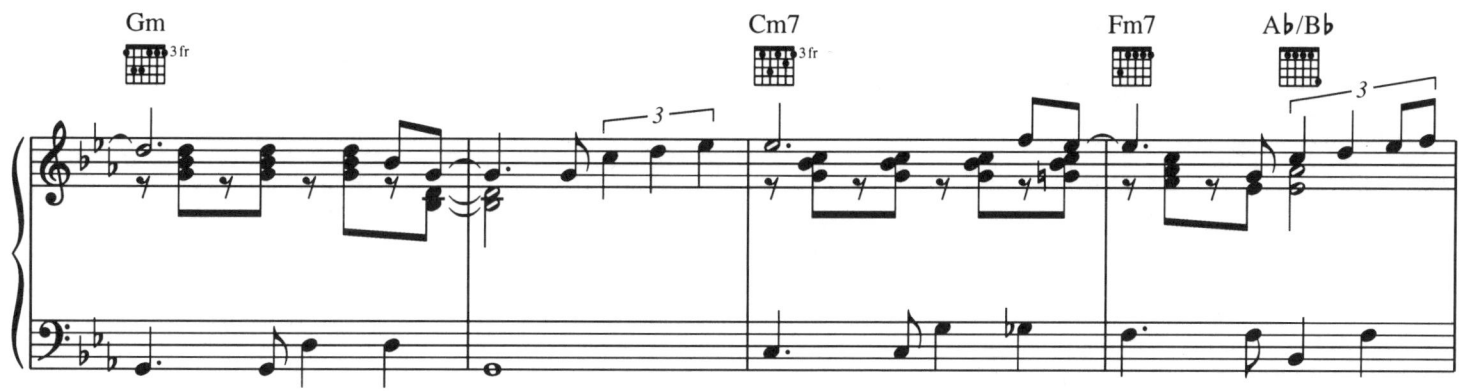
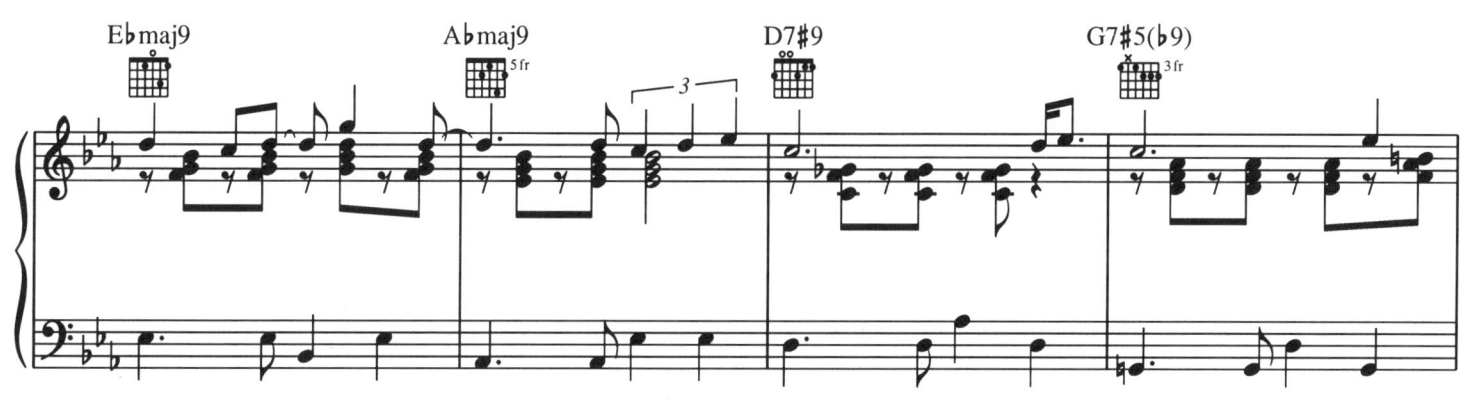
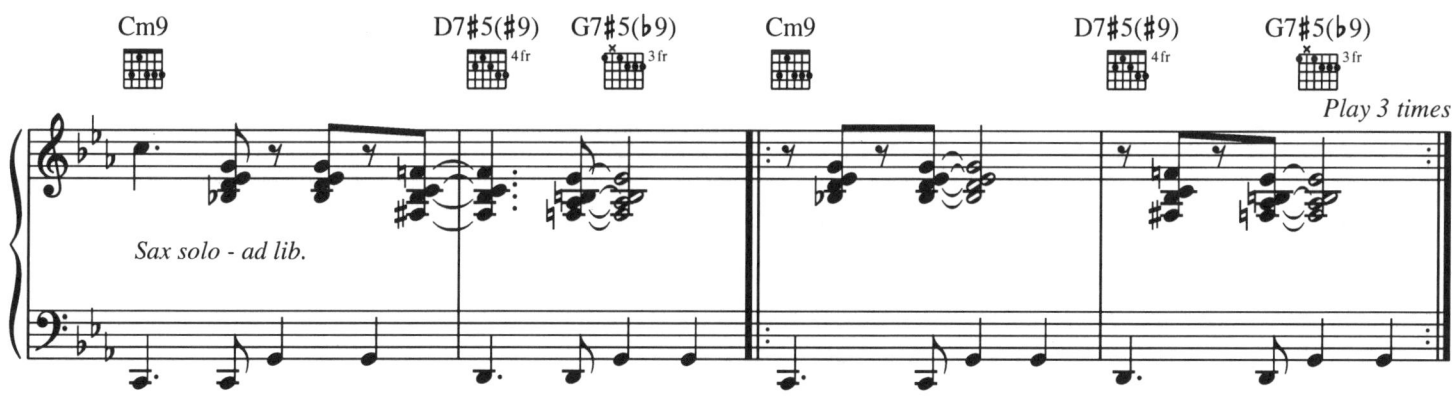
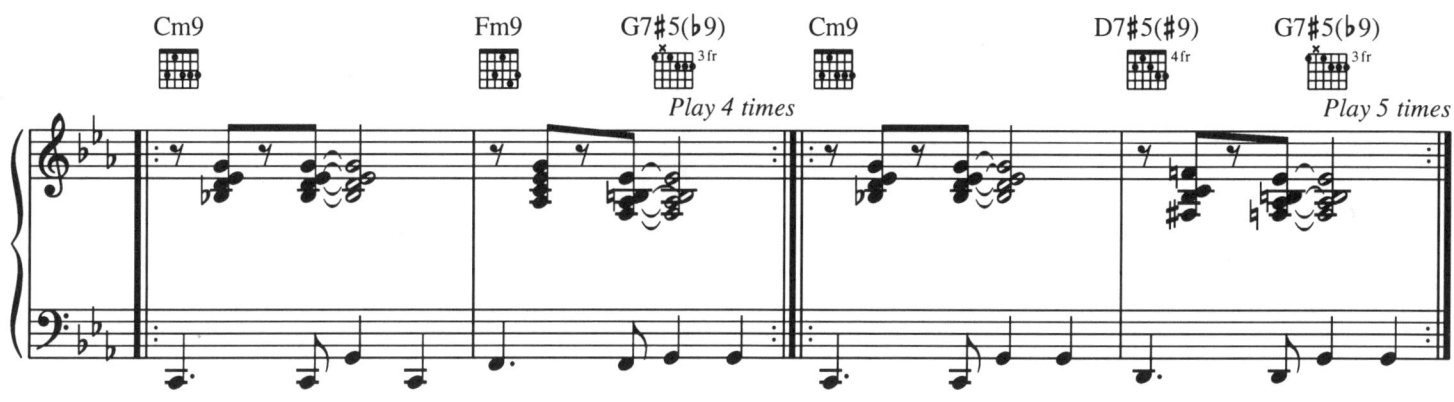

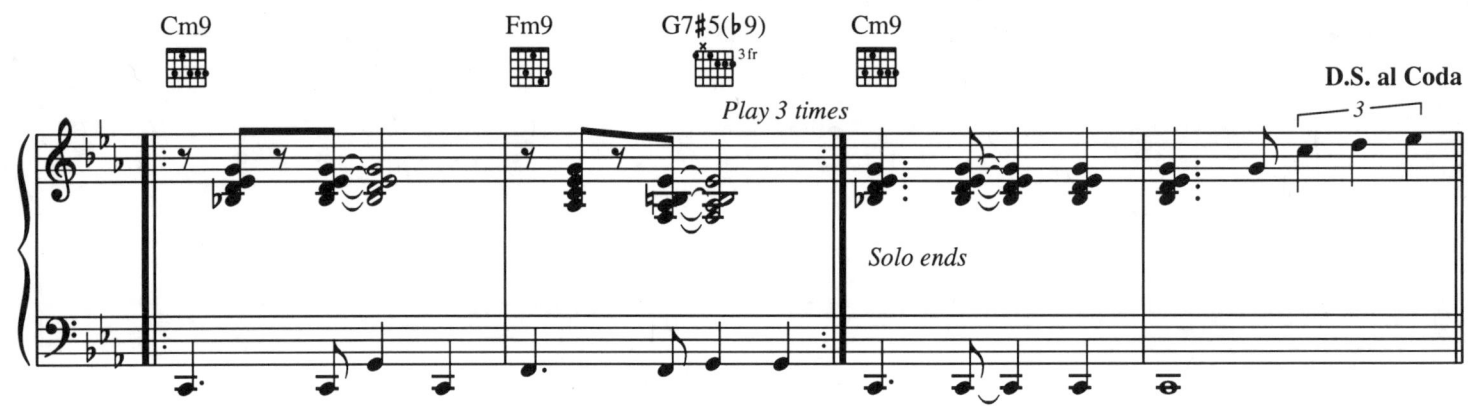
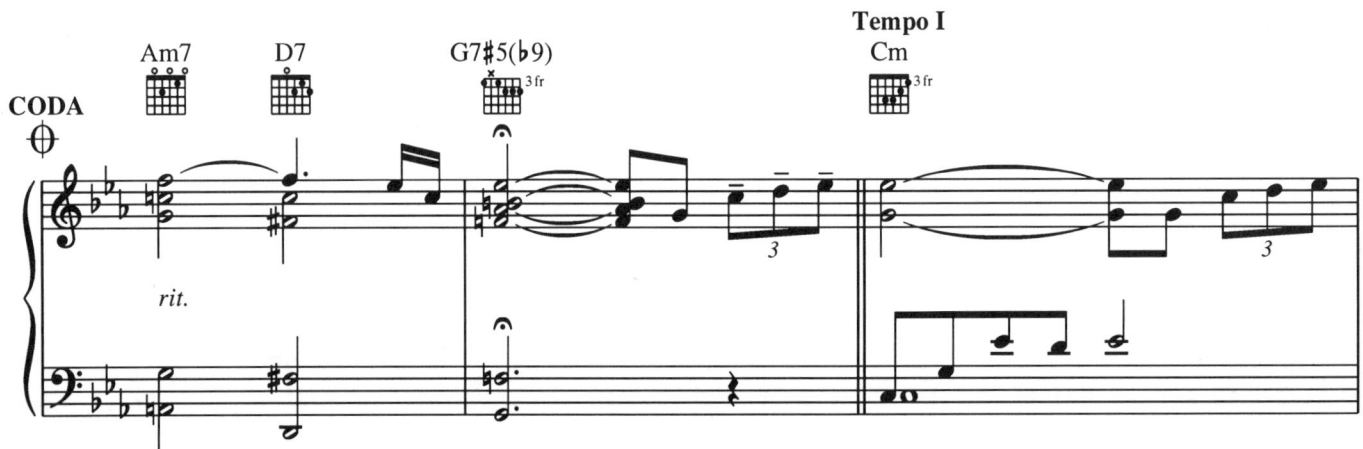
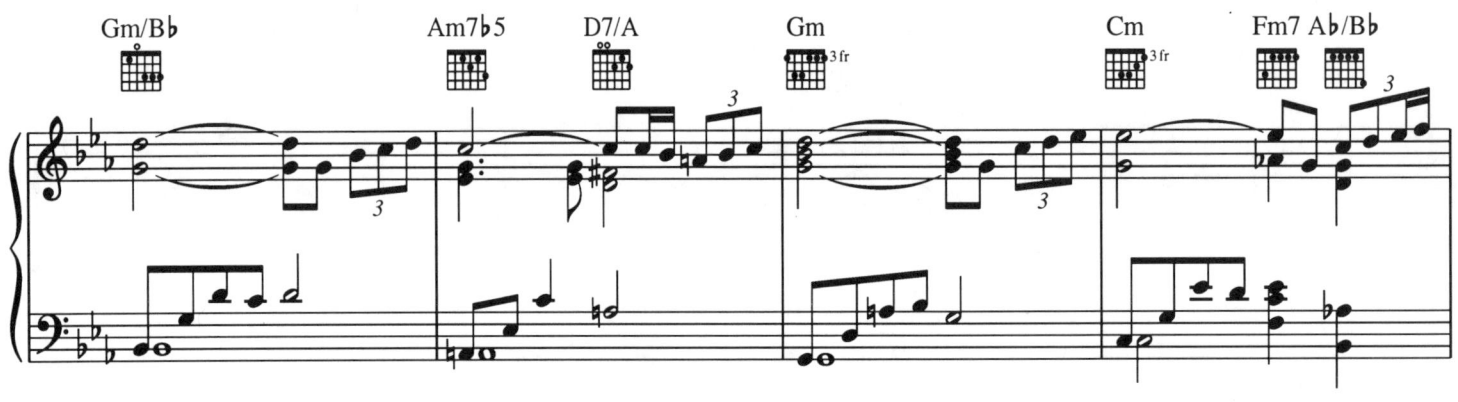
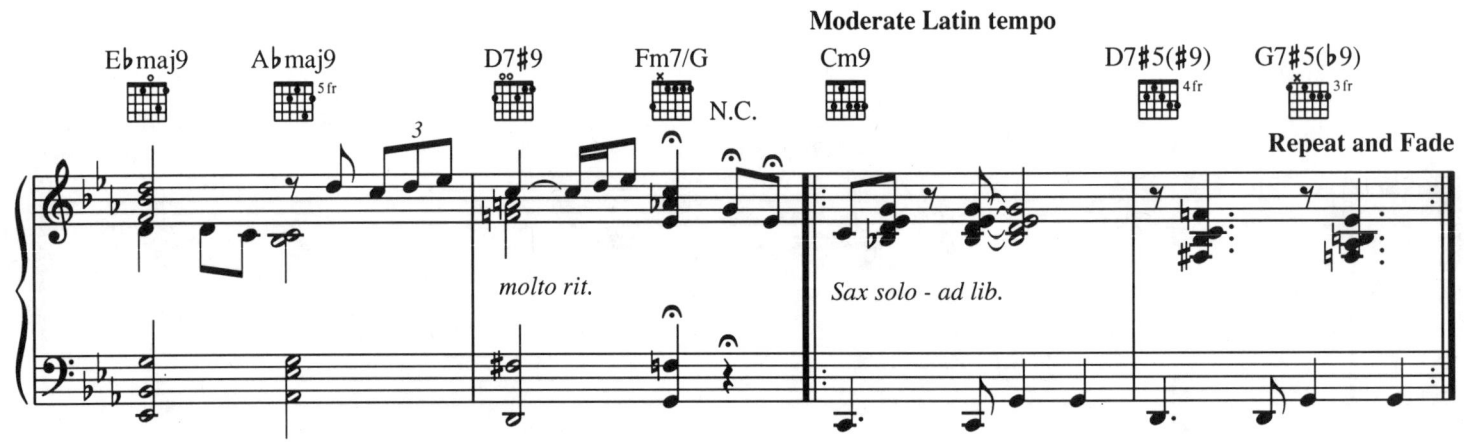

BY THE TIME THIS NIGHT IS OVER

Words and Music by MICHAEL BOLTON,
ANDY GOLDMARK and DIANE WARREN

BABY G

By KENNY G, WALTER AFANASIEFF and DAN SHEA

© 1997 KENNY G MUSIC, SONY/ATV TUNES LLC, WALLYWORLD MUSIC and PICNIC HILL MUSIC
All Rights on behalf of SONY/ATV TUNES LLC and WALLYWORLD MUSIC Administered by SONY/ATV MUSIC PUBLISHING, 8 Music Square West, Nashville, TN 37203
International Copyright Secured   All Rights Reserved

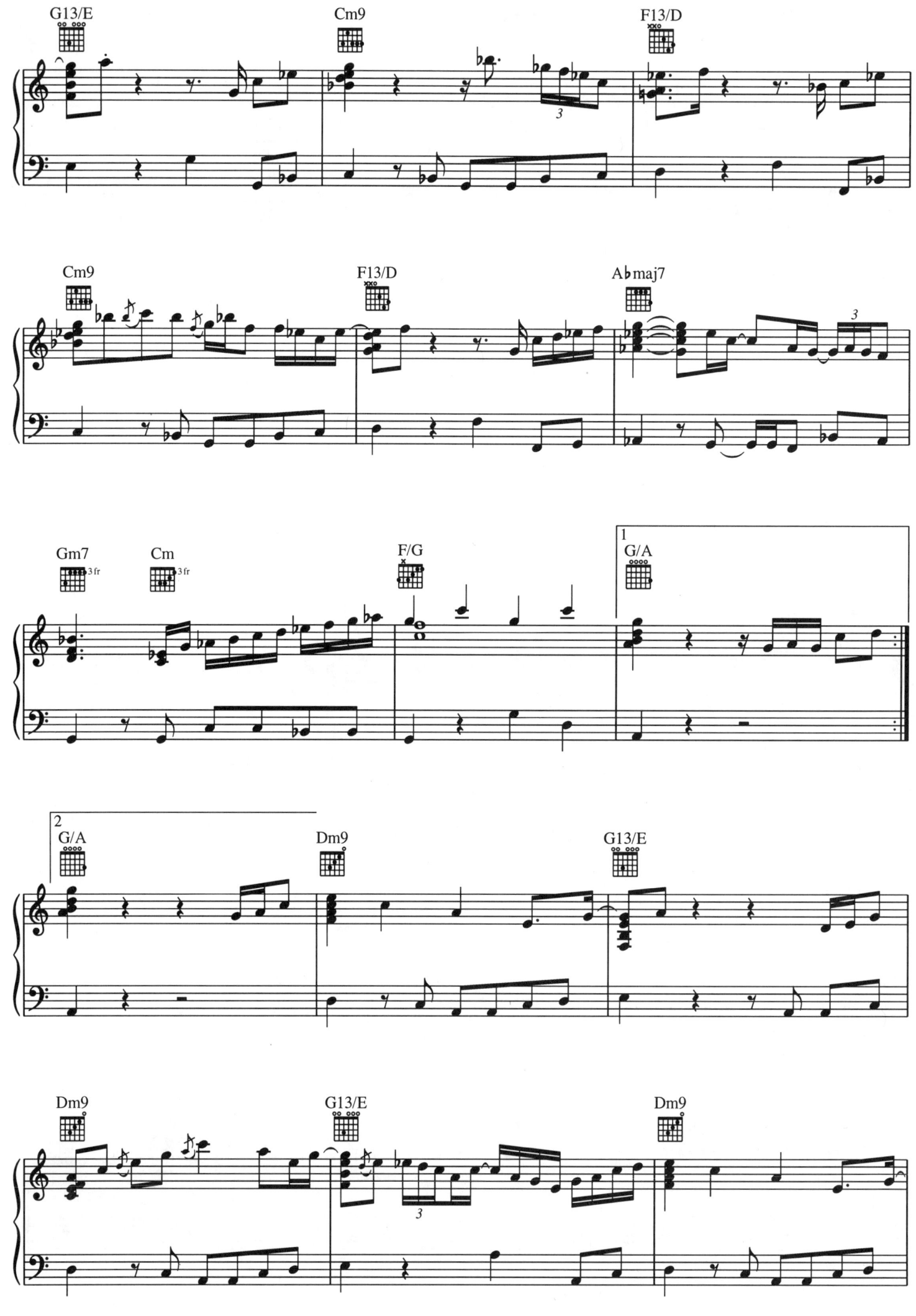

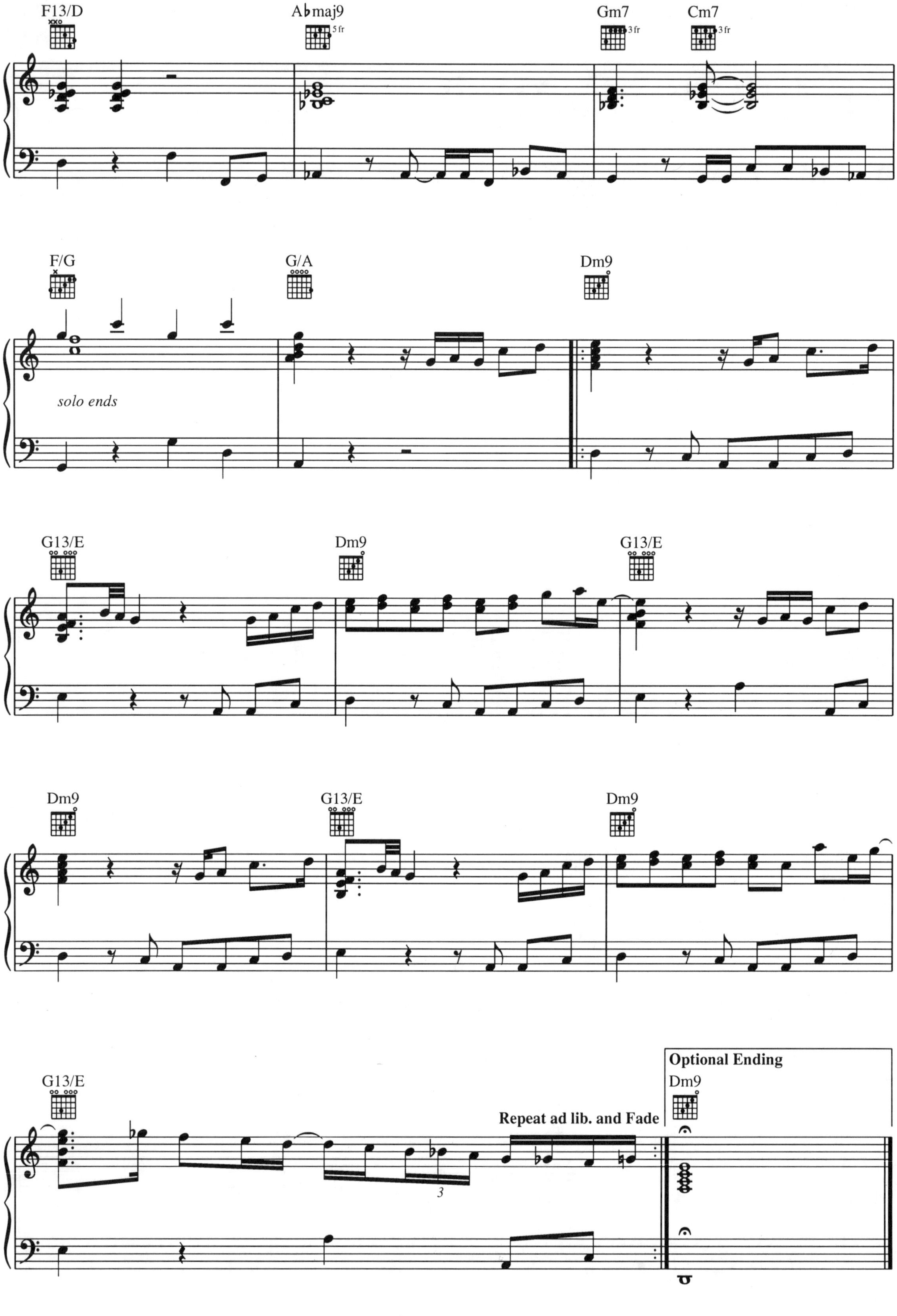
F13/D
A♭maj9
Gm7
Cm7
F/G
G/A
Dm9
solo ends
G13/E
Dm9
G13/E
Dm9
G13/E
Dm9
G13/E
Repeat ad lib. and Fade
Optional Ending
Dm9

THEME FROM DYING YOUNG

Music by
JAMES NEWTON HOWARD

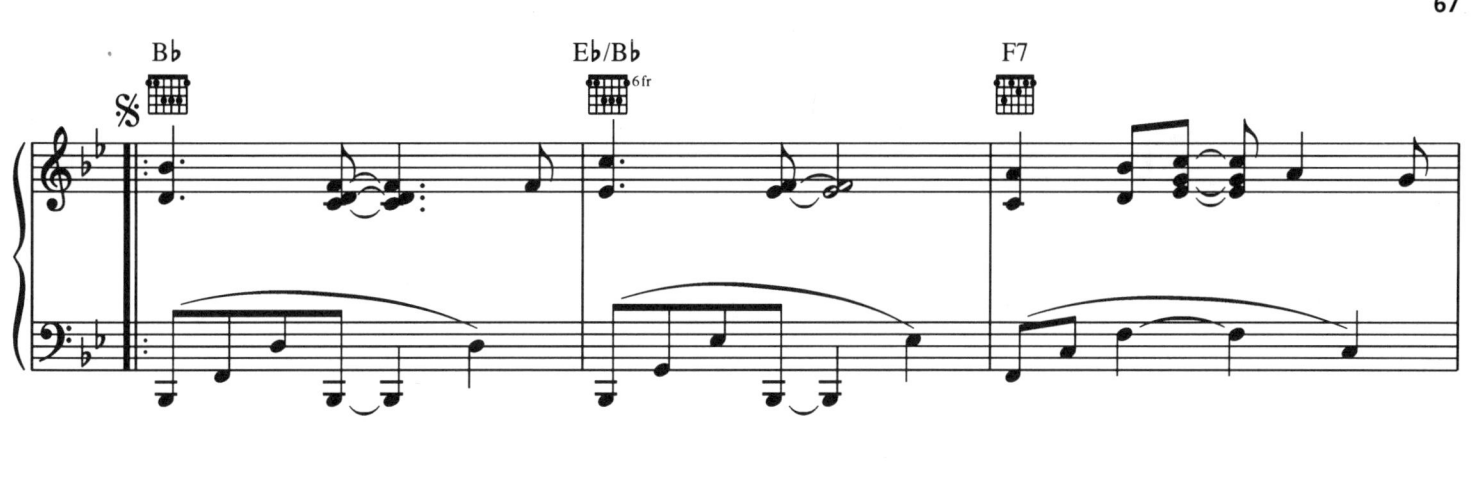
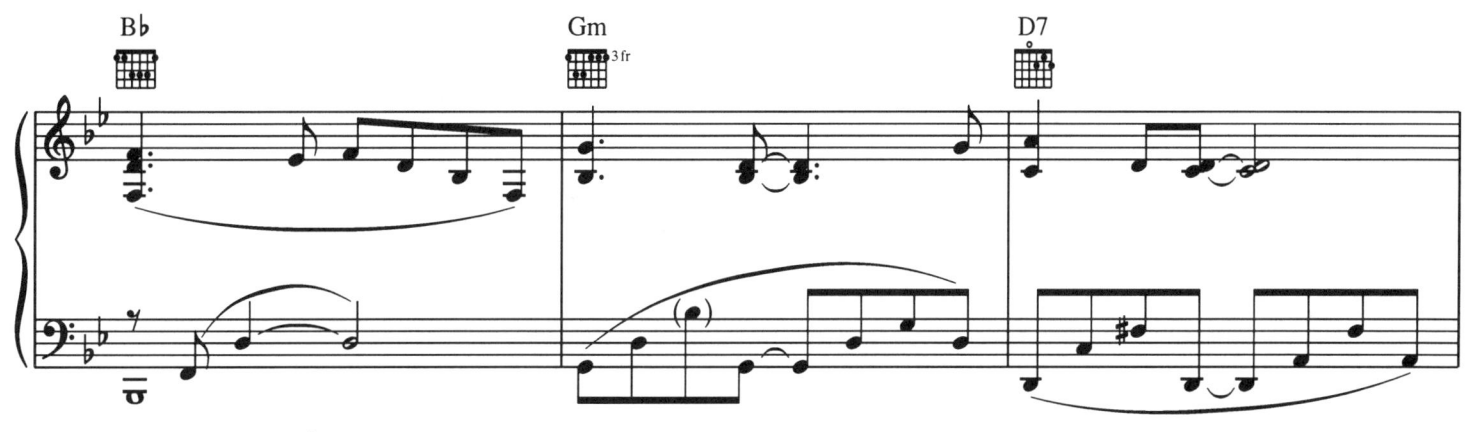
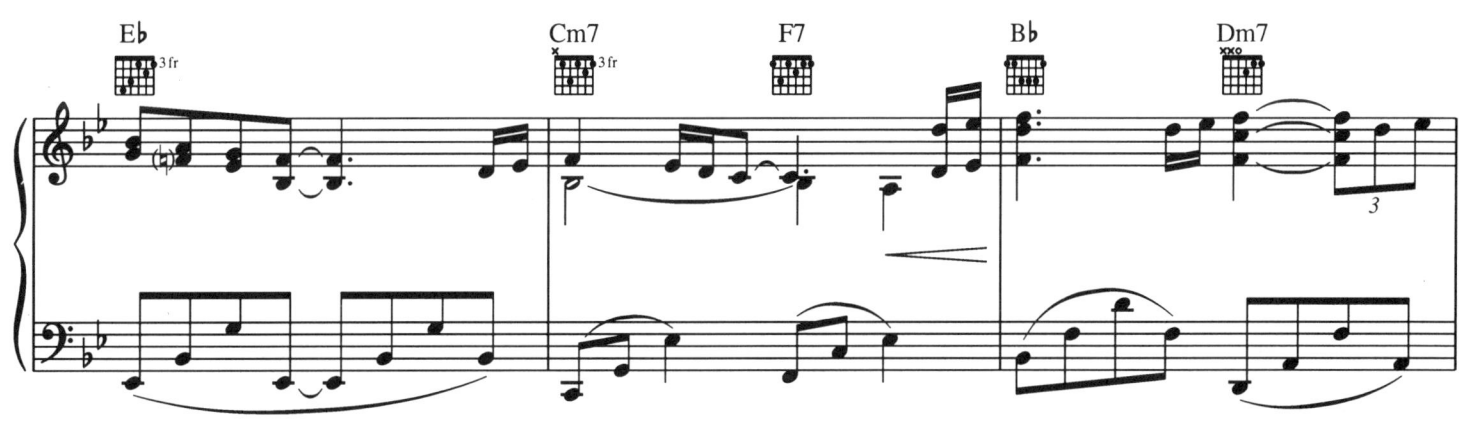
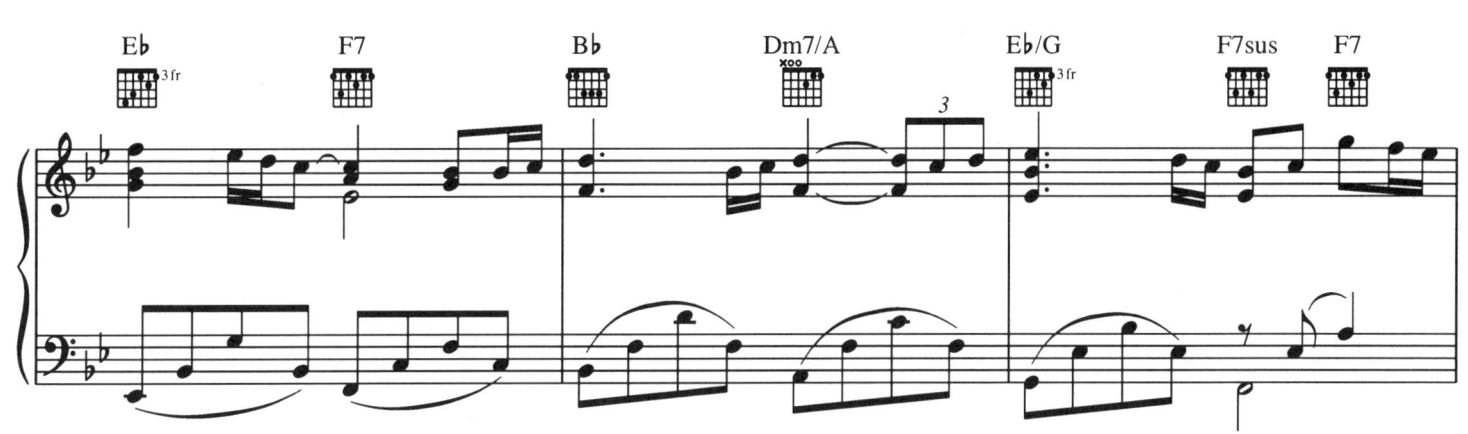

68

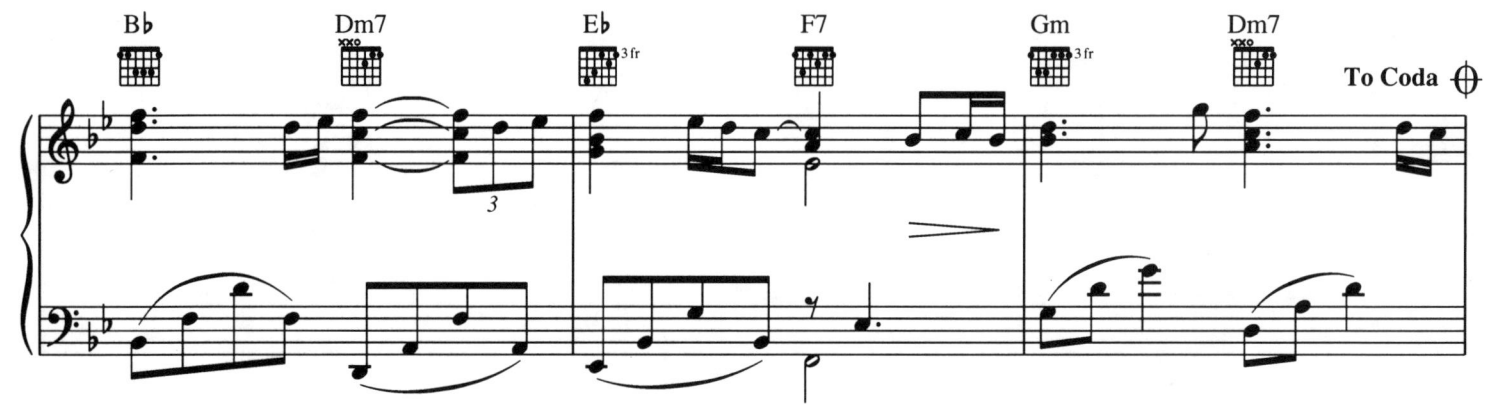

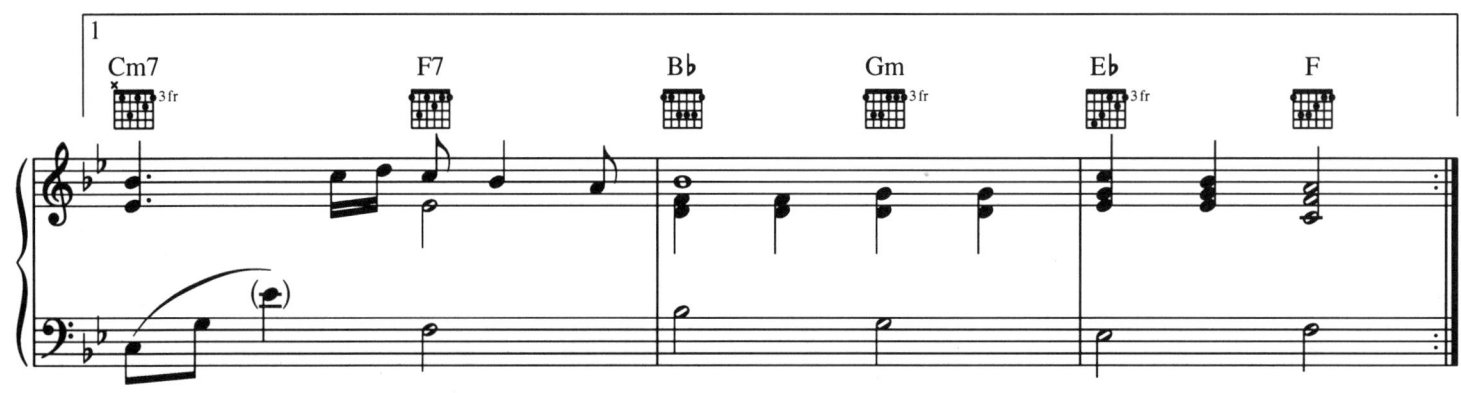

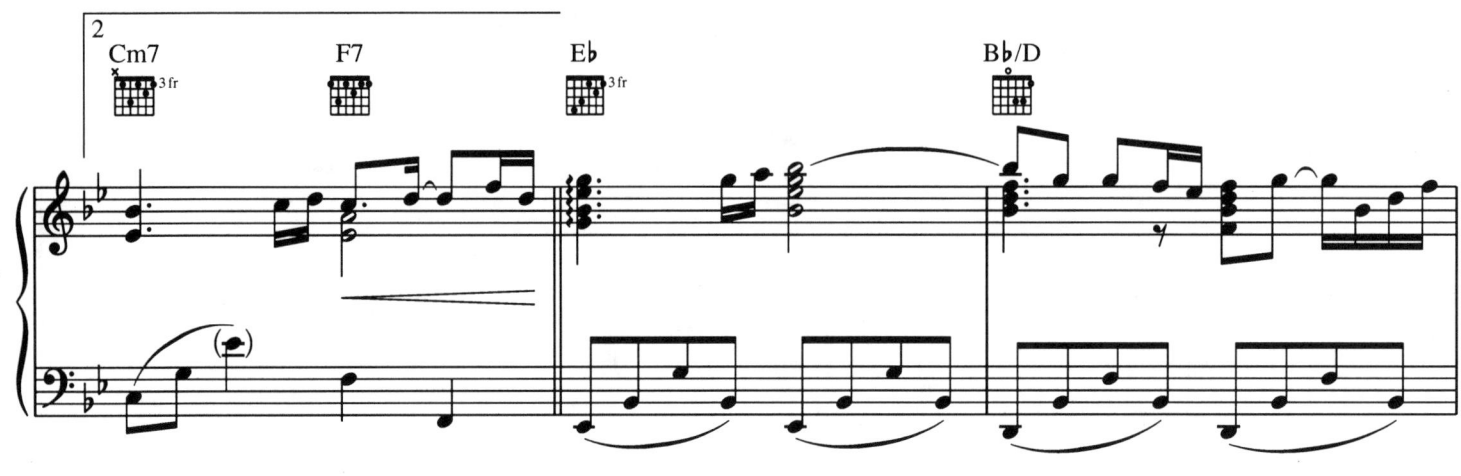

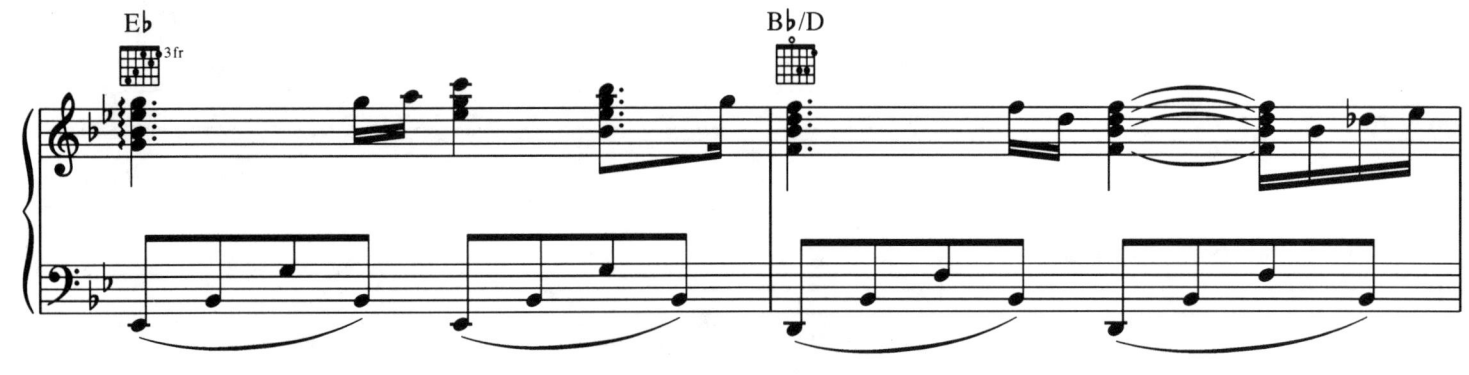

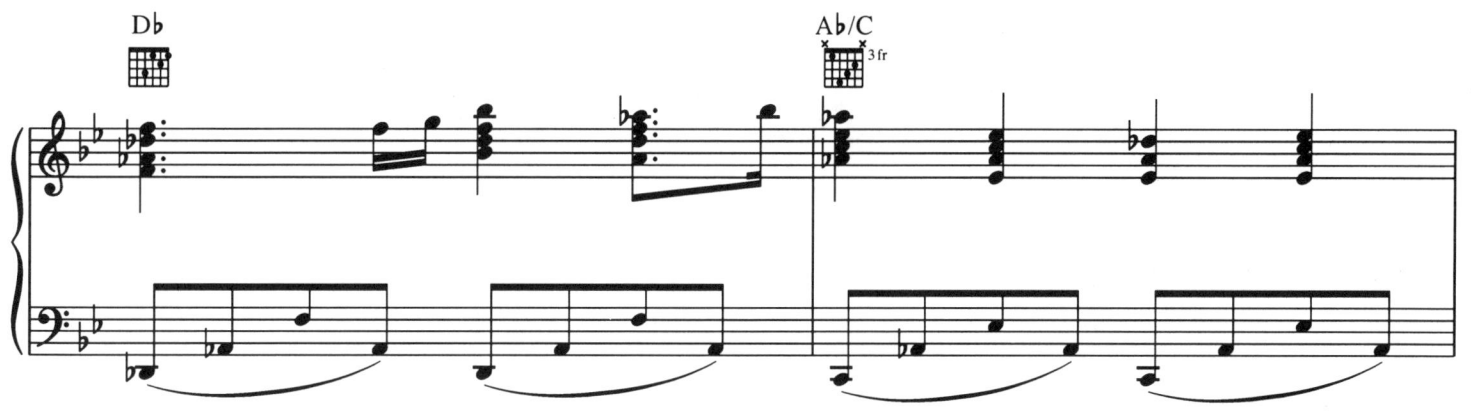
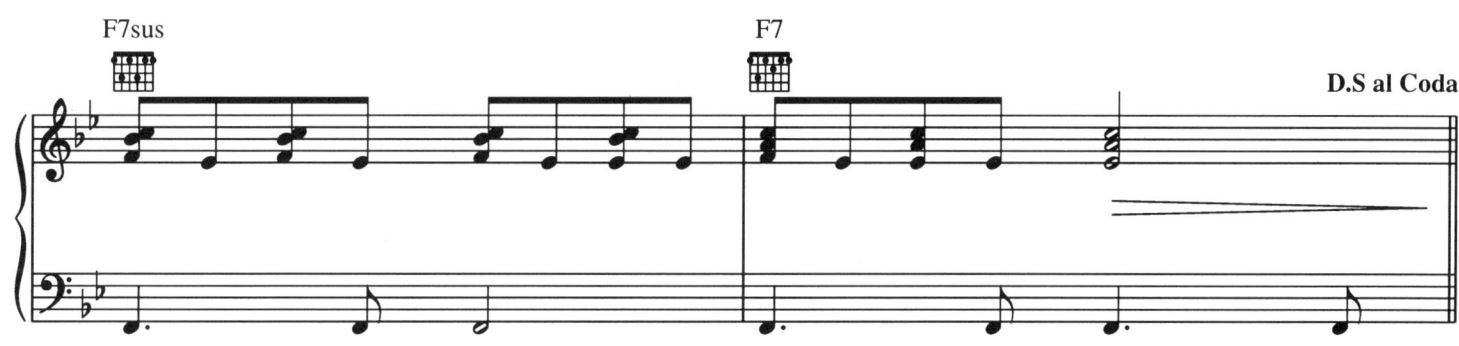
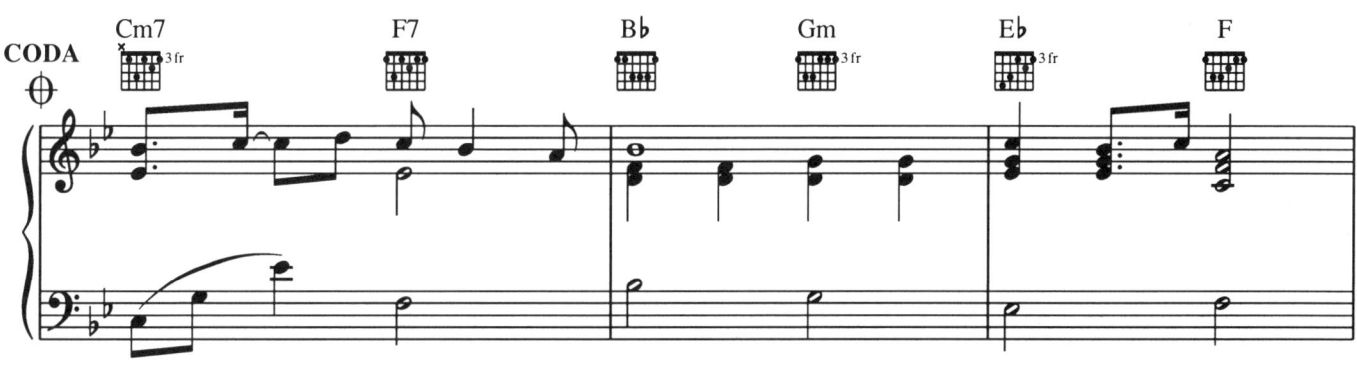
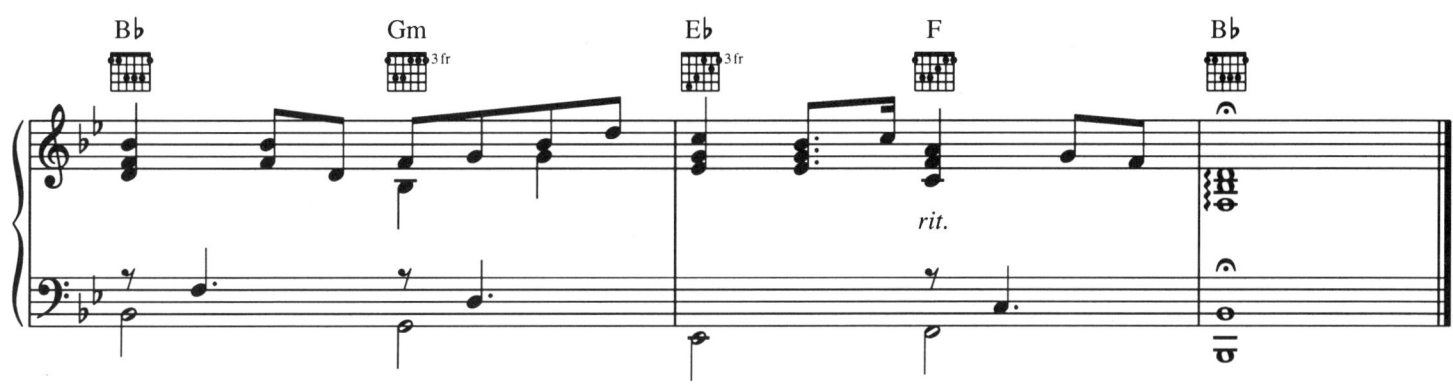

76

INNOCENCE

By KENNY G and WALTER AFANASIEFF